How Many Covered Bridges

There are various rules to determine if a bridge with a roof over it is recognized by certain institutions as a covered bridge. In Oregon, the Legislature set up a "Covered Bridge Maintenance and Rehabilitation Program (Oregon Laws Chapter 722), which defines covered bridges as "housed, load bearing single-span wooden truss bridges." Repair work on these can be covered by state funds if available. Under this law, 44 covered bridges in Oregon quality.

Some specific housed bridges are omitted from the "accepted" list (Rock o' the Range, Milo Academy, Lake Creek, Cedar Crossing). Although these bridges are "housed," they have girders, concrete slabs, or steel support trusses as their main supports and do not qualify for state-paid rehabilitation. Drift Creek bridge is omitted as it was demolished with about half its parts salvaged as re-usable, those moved to a new site. Its new "house" will rest on a concrete slab.

For the purpose of this book, *Oregon Covered Bridges – Expanded Edition* (1999), includes all bridges verified and accessible to the public by the editors in Oregon that are roofed regardless of the style of construction and regardless if publicly or privately owned, vehicular or walking only.

This book identifies 65 covered bridges in Oregon including Widing Covered Bridge which was recently demolished by real estate developers. Our book does not list covered bridges on golf courses.

For a list of covered bridges by county, turn to page 100. Our Master List of covered bridges we have verified in Oregon is on page 108. The Table of Contents, page *v*, lists bridges alphabetically by name.

Oregon Covered Bridges

Dedication

Fred Kildow

Fred Kildow, a native of Oregon, is acknowledged by "bridgers" nationwide as the Dean of Oregon covered bridges. Fred was one of the founders of the Covered Bridge Society of Oregon in 1978 and was the society's first president (1979-81). He was later corresponding secretary for many years and his address has been used as a stability point for the group for years "as others come and go."

Kildow has been interested in covered bridges since the 1930's when he drove through some of them in his Model T Ford. He became seriously interested in 1971 when he read a sign that had been tacked to the wall of Lost Creek Covered Bridge in Jackson County. The little poster had been put there by a visitor from the Northern Ohio Covered Bridge society.

When Fred Kildow was on a trip to Ohio in 1972, he and his party stopped a road repair crew and asked if there might be a covered bridge nearby. The men gave directions to three. On viewing them, Fred adopted covered bridges as his No. 1 hobby.

In 1945 Fred married Mary DiSanto. He and Mary parented and enjoy four children and presently have five grandchildren. They live in a suburb of southwest Portland where their home is decorated with every kind of artwork relating to covered bridges.

It is with pride that we dedicate this book to

Fred Kildow
Dean of Oregon Covered Bridges

Webb Research Group Publishers of books about the Oregon Country

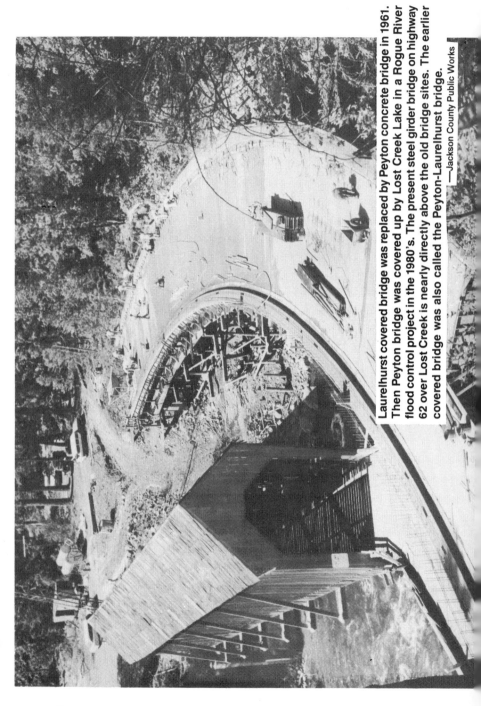

Laurelhurst covered bridge was replaced by Peyton concrete bridge in 1961. Then Peyton bridge was covered up by Lost Creek Lake in a Rogue River flood control project in the 1980's. The present steel girder bridge on highway 62 over Lost Creek is nearly directly above the old bridge sites. The earlier covered bridge was also called the Peyton-Laurelhurst bridge.

—Jackson County Public Works

Oregon

Covered

Bridges

DOCUMENTARY

Expanded Edition

6 New Bridges
Not In Earlier Books
Where To See Them

Bert and Margie Webber

Webb Research Group Publishers
Books About the Oregon Country

Please direct all inquiries to the Publisher:

WEBB RESEARCH GROUP PUBLISHERS
Books About the Oregon Country
P. O. Box 314
Medford, Oregon 97501

The six new covered bridges
mentioned on the title page are:

Cascadia (page 21)
Dave Birtch Dam (page 34)
Joel Whittemore (page 52)
Mott Memorial (page 65)
Porter–Limpy Creek (page 88)
Wayne A. Perry (page 92)

Drift Creek Covered Bridge shown on page 37 was
demolished and rebuilt on Bear Creek. Reopened Summer 1999

Jordan Covered Bridge shown on page 54
has been rebuilt on site and was dedicated in September 1998.
It is now called the **Stayton-Jordan Covered Bridge**.

Roaring Camp Covered Bridge on pages 10, 79-80
was dismantled in 1995 and replaced with a steel span.

The **Widing Covered Bridge** shown on pages 96-97 was
dismantled and developers reclaimed the swampy
area for construction. No trace of the bridge remains.

The picture on the Title Page is the old Howe truss
Mill Creek Covered Bridge
built in 1910 south of Buell, Polk County. The bridge was 100-
feet long and 15-feet 8-inches wide. Bridge no longer stands.
—Photo from Oregon Department of Transportation

Library of Congress Cataloging-in-Publication Data:

Webber, Bert.
    Oregon covered bridges / Bert and Margie Webber. – Expanded ed.
        p.   cm.
    Includes bibliographical references and index
    ISBN 0-936738-86-3
    1. Covered bridges—Oregon.   I. Webber, Margie. II. Title.
TG24.07W43   1995
624'.37'09795—dc20   95-12050
                    [Published Spring 1999]   CIP

Contents

Photographing Covered Bridges

Our professional cameramen comment that a picture of a single covered bridge does not usually present a challenge for finding a suitable camera angle. Just point-and-shoot. But if the person expects to photograph a number of covered bridges, it might be a good idea to consider a series of different angles.

The pitfall, in photographing covered bridges, is the risk of sameness. This is to stand in front of the portal (end) of the bridge and just push the shutter button. What is the result other than a picture of a barn with big, gaping holes in the ends? But covered bridges are unique because they are boxes with holes in their ends.

Consider: Do close-up pictures of bridge portals make a good photograph of the <u>bridge</u>, or does the photo yield only a picture of a big, dark blob?

The best pictures are made on bright, sunny days.

Looking at some examples in this book to avoid "sameness," consider these:

> **While stumbling through the underbrush seeking good camera angles, be alert that there are probably TICKS waiting to grab you on the way by.**

Cavitt – Catch both ends of the pointed arch portals by standing back away from the bridge.

Cedar Crossing – This is a flash picture at night but at long time exposure to pick up the inside lighting. Tripod recommended.

Centennial – High angle from nearby building. This is a "3/4-front."

Chambers – Low angle and slightly off-center.

China Ditch – 3/4-front. Photographed on black & white film with dark yellow filter to darken sky.

Chitwood – Low angle and 3/4-front. Effective use of late afternoon shadow. With b&w film, add a dark yellow filter.

Eagle Point – Aerial at 1/200th Sec. on b&w film with dark yellow filter.

Fourtner – Very low angle, 3/4-side.

Gilkey – 3/4-front, low angle, b&w film, dark yellow filter.

Grave Creek – Effective use of signs.

Hannah – Put a person doing something in the view. Note effective use of signs.

Harris – A big, happy dog brings life to an otherwise static scene on a "dead (no sun) day."

McKee – High angle. Photographer stood in bed of high pickup truck.

Mosby Creek / Short / Tissot / Porter / Widing – Effective use of foliage.

→The expense of a trip is <u>getting to a covered bridge</u>, not the cost of the film. Shoot plenty while you are there and change angles often!
　　　　　　　　　　　　　　　　　　—Bert Webber, Research Photojournalist

Goodpasture Covered Bridge, McKenzie River May 1983. "Ten minutes later it rained – buckets – and the bridge was glad it had its hat on."
—Glenn Barkhurst photo

Many beautiful gorges in Oregon mountains needed bridges to hook the ends of the roads together. This scene is near the source of the Rogue River. The best place to obtain lumber for these bridges was among the heavy stands of timber close to the bridge sites. This harvest thinned the forest to provide a more healthy environment for the forest. This was years before studies of sustained yield, tree farms and mention of spotted owls which often lived in the rafters of the covered bridges.

This photograph was made from a concrete span that replaced a covered bridge about one mile south of Prospect in Jackson County.
—Bert Webber photo

Covered Bridges Are All Around Us

Covered bridges are often associated with fond personal memories, or with vicarious wonderment for those who have never seen one or driven across one. Covered bridges are claimed, after lighthouses, as being for tourists, the most often photographed man-made objects. Artists, particularly in New England, have had a field day with their drawings of covered bridges which have received wide circulation on calendars and greeting cards. Therefore, many people associate covered bridges with New England. Regrettably, many fine folks have not anticipated that these wonders exist elsewhere. In some states, there are great numbers.

> A tally made in 1989, indicates the greatest
> number of covered bridges were found in:
> Europe
>   Switzerland 183
>   Germany 119
>   Austria 93
> United States
>   Pennsylvania 222
>   Ohio 141
>   Vermont 102
>   Indiana 93
>   New Hampshire 54
>   Oregon 53
>   –Source: *World Guide to Covered Bridges*

In Oregon, the first covered bridge, that we can trace, was completed in 1851. It was in Oregon City. This was a bridge that extended from Main Street to Abernethy Island in the Willamette River. Another covered bridge had been started in 1850 in Lafayette, over the North Fork of the Yamhill River, but is was 1852 before this was finished. Regrettably, the floods of 1853 took out both of these early covered bridges.

The longest *standing* covered bridge in Oregon is the Drift Creek Covered Bridge in Lincoln County – 1914. As to how

Bert Webber with historic sign that had earlier been mounted near the bridge. The worn out Roaring Camp Covered Bridge was dismantled in 1995 and re-placed with a steel span. — Gene Olson photo

many covered bridges there have been in Oregon, the only list that has been located was one done by the former Oregon State Highway Department titled *Index of Covered Bridges in Oregon – 1947.* This appeared in 1948. On that list, the dates of construction are simply stated as "date unknown" for 199 bridges. The only known recent reprint appears as an Appendix in *Oregon Covered* Bridges (1991).

There are recognizable errors. For Jackson County, records show that the Hartman Brothers, covered bridge specialists, built or worked on 27 bridges. According to an article in the Medford *Mail Tribune*, (July 19, 1954), the brothers named 8 bridges standing at that time. But the state list shows only 5.

Of the covered bridges standing today throughout Oregon, most were built between 1910 and 1950. Of those we found, recorded by decades are:

1910 - 1919	6	1960 - 1969	5
1920 - 1929	18	1970 - 1979	–
1930 - 1939*	19	1980 - 1989	7
1940 - 1949**	6	1990 -	3
1950 - 1959	1		

*Jordan (1937) burned 1994, rebuilt 1998
**Bohemian Hall (1947) moved to be rebuilt

Total 65

Rochester Covered Bridge February 1995   —Bert Webber photo

The Light At The End Of The Tunnel

"I begin to feel that the horror may move away and that there is a big round spot of real daylight at the end of the tunnel."   — J. Middleton Murray (1922)

In the present decade, three were built in 1990. These were in Arlington, Gilliam County, and in Wolf Creek, Josephine County. The most recent to come to our attention, built in 1991, is near Williams in Josephine County.

There is argument among the stoutest of the covered bridge *aficionados* as to what constitutes a genuine covered bridge. It is generally agreed that the bridge should be mostly constructed of wood, at least from the deck upward. (How about from the deck down?) Some say the bridge needs to have timber trusses to support the weight of the bridge and its passing load. In some engineering designs, metal tension rods in the trusses are recognized. Many of the conservative thinkers believe the sides and roofing needs to be of wood. But there are many examples of corrugated sheet-iron on roofs and some with sheet metal siding. Some have no siding at all.

A "legitimate" covered bridge is one that, when built, was to be used for vehicles with decks eight or more feet wide and that the bridge serve a worthwhile purpose. This might be the crossing of a stream – any size – maybe a gulch where there was a spring runoff, a railroad or a ravine. A minimum length for a covered bridge does not seem to have been in dispute for there are some very short covered bridges that meet the general guidelines.

The matter of construction principles creeps into the specifications. Early-on, covered bridges were of a certain "truss" design. But more recent covered bridges have departed from the truss in favor of expedient modern substitutions. The **Rock O' The Range** bridge is a "Timber Deck Girder." **Widing** and **Wolf Creek** are "Frame Stringers." **Cedar Crossing** is an asphalt deck with Glulam stringers. **China Ditch** and **Warner Canyon** are built on old railroad flatcars. A bridge, even with a roof over it, may be listed merely as a "roofed span." **Cedar Crossing** and **China Ditch** meets this distinction. How does one list a concrete span with a lid? **Milo Academy** and new **Drift Creek** are these.

For oddities to the so-called "norm," how about a deck on the *roof*, with vehicles driving on the roof? For examples, look in this book for **Cascadia** and **Mott Memorial**.

It should be said that for the purpose of this book, cute little covered bridges intended for golf carts on golf courses, of which there are a great many, are not discussed or included.

This is the third of three books on covered bridges by the authors. Each book is related yet substantially different. They have the same title, *Oregon Covered Bridges* except the present book is officially registered as *Expanded Edition*. This is because the new book shows six more covered bridges than were listed earlier. In the first book (1991) are many pages of specialized matter. These include photographs of bridges in art. The selection also offers outstanding drawings on flower bowls, pot holders, and saw blades. There is pine needle raffia, and designs burnt in wood. There are oil paintings on china, punch needle wall hanging, etc. That book includes the Oregon State Department of Transportation's Covered Bridge Preservation plans. In that volume is also found the only printed list (since 1948) of the official *Index of Covered Bridges in Oregon - 1947*. This *Index* lists the bridges in the state's history by county. Readers desiring to

Oregon – The "Last Bastion"

"Oregon is the last bastion of covered bridges in the west," wrote Burrell Smith, a member of the Covered Bridge Society of Oregon. He continued, "Covered bridges are a tourist attraction as well as a source of pride for all Oregonians.

"Oregon ranks fifth in having the most covered bridges in the United States. Only Pennsylvania, Ohio, Vermont and New Hampshire have more." California and Washington have just a few left. — *The Bridge Tender.* Vol. 14. No. 3. Fall 1993.

study this historical material are referred to the 1991 edition. Persons might contact the publisher, whose address is on page *iv,* to determine if sales copies are still available. Another source is to inquire at public libraries. If approaching a librarian, specify "the 1991 edition."

*   *   *

The authors are indebted to many fine people who collaborated with us during the research stage of this project. Frederick Kildow, dean of the Oregon covered bridge enthusiasts, always entertained our inquiries with friendly enthusiasm and he continues to do so for the present volume.

Steve Webber, a nephew, who was Archivist of the City of Portland at the time of early research, went with us to rediscover what we called "Oregon's lost covered bridge" – the **Widing** – which had become so heavily entangled in a jungle of wild blackberries, it was easy for the passerby to miss.

We acknowledge the friendly assistance of Mike Kieffer, Region 3 Bridge Inspector of the Oregon Department of Transportation (Roseburg), for his knowledge of the history of covered bridges and for his up-to-the-minute remarks as to conditions on various bridges. We also thank Peter Pagner, Salem, a bridge design engineer, who is also with ODOT.

Although the authors have been quietly collecting and studying covered bridges as far back as 1941, they welcome the aquaintance of John Snook, Medford. John is a senior citizen whose hobby has been photographing Oregon covered bridges. Many of his pictures have been included. We appreciate his fine camera work and helpful attitude.

There were many other individuals who offered input. These include Orville Erdman, Bandon; Ben Dahlenburg, Sweethome;

Kay West, Arlington; Judy Hillman, Salem; Bob Pepperling, Canada; Morris X. Smith, Chitwood; Don and Evelyn Porter, Grants Pass; Merle and Susan Converse, Wolf Creek; Wayne and Jane Perry, Williams; Dave and Tammie Birtch, Dillard; Laura Sweitz, Drift Creek.

We acknowledge the fine work of Bill Cockrell, who did an earlier book on these bridges, and who is the editor of the notable periodical, *The Bridge Tender,* published by the Covered Bridge Society of Oregon. This high-quality quarterly magazine contains feature stories about the various Oregon covered bridges. If a bridge is damaged, rebuilt, repainted, or when a new bridge is constructed, articles usually appear about these matters. Readers interested in learning about the society can write to the publisher (address on page iv) for information.

Of significance in all of our writing projects is that we recognize the need for professional library research. Of great help is the staff at Jackson County Library Services, Main Medford Branch. The several Reference Librarians individually received our thanks.

We are aware that in spite of our research and editing care, some readers may feel they have different information or have spotted an error. This edition is a revision of the 1995 book. Constructive criticism is invited and may be sent to the publisher at the address on page *iv*.

Bert and Margie Webber
Central Point, Oregon
Winter 1998-1999

There is a "STATUS" check-box for each bridge. Be aware that status often changes without notice. Many times, a bridge may be closed to all traffic due to emergency or temporary repair but a bridge may be barricaded for only a few hours for a special inspection. The Preservation Program arranges for minor and major repairs which may cause major changes to the Status.

STATUS:	
CLOSED	☑
Status subject to change	

STATUS	
OPEN TO:	
VEHICLES	☑
WALKERS	☑
BIKERS	☑
Status subject to change	

STATUS	
OPEN TO:	
WALKERS	☑
BIKERS	☑
Status subject to change	

14

KING POST

(WOOD)
TRADITIONAL TRUSS
ORIGIN IN THE MIDDLE AGES

LENGTH 20-60 FEET
(6-18 METERS)

QUEEN POST

(WOOD)
LENGTHENED VERSION OF THE
KING POST

LENGTH 20-80 FEET
(6-24 METERS)

Trusses

Truss: A supporting frame or structure especially in the construction of
a roof or bridge.

— *Encyclopædia Britannica* 11th Ed. 1910

No discussion about covered bridges can be complete
without some understanding of the word "truss." As a verb,
"truss" indicates what a chef does to a chicken or turkey
before roasting it. As a noun, "truss" is a scientific contri-
bution of the Renaissance. Andrea Palladio, a 16th Century
architect, is credited with designing an arrangement of a
rigid triangle in wood – a truss. He put together what we
today recognize as the "Kingpost" and the "Queenpost"
truss bridges.

The Kingpost is the simplest form. It consists of a center
post framed into two triangles by a bottom chord. A major
drawback to the Kingpost is that for a very heavy load,
longer (higher) diagonals must be used. As what we now
call "old growth timber" was not available at the time, the
solution was to maintain a low profile by adding more
diagonals but, in so doing, the centers had no support.
Accordingly, the Queenpost was the answer. This was a
"stretched" version of two Kingposts joined together with a
horizontal rail or "chord."

At this writing, the only true Kingpost covered bridge in
Oregon is the Neal Lane bridge in Douglas County. This is a

relatively short length bridge and has a restricted load – 5 tons.

(*Britannica* points out that in 1910, the engineering strongly suggested that a 30-foot length was all a Kingpost could handle.)

In Josephine County, the newer Wayne A. Perry Covered Bridge (1991) uses modified Kingpost construction.

As illustrated in our chart, the Kingpost is usable up to 60-feet length. The Queenpost can handle up to 80-feet. These are assumed to be relatively low-profile structures as with the covered bridges in Oregon.

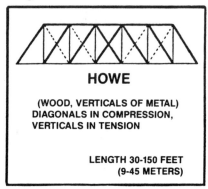

HOWE

(WOOD, VERTICALS OF METAL)
DIAGONALS IN COMPRESSION,
VERTICALS IN TENSION

LENGTH 30-150 FEET
(9-45 METERS)

For a unique application of the Howe Truss, see the Chambers Covered Bridge.

The Howe Truss came about in 1840 when William Howe used metal rods he called "tension bolts" to provide extra support. The rods are like giant screws as they are threaded and have nuts to fit. The tension can be adjusted with a giant wheel wrench that often took up to six men, all applying their strength simultaneously to the wheel to tighten. When the tension was correct on all of the rods on a bridge, the bridge did not sag.

There are five Queenpost covered bridges in Oregon:

> Lost Creek - Jackson County
> Eagle Point - Jackson County
> Wimer - Jackson County
> North Fork Yachats River - Lincoln County
> Fourtner - Polk County

Queenpost truss within the Eagle Point Covered Bridge

In the 1988 study by the Oregon Department of Transportation, prepared as a report for the 1989 legislature, two other trusses are mentioned:

Steel girder	Milo Academy - Douglas County
Deck Girder	Rock O' the Range - Deschutes County
	Cedar Crossing - Multnomah County

There were many other patented truss designs in the early days of covered bridge building. We list them here for reference, but none are seen in any of the covered bridges in Oregon today.

Burr Arch; Multiple Kingpost; Arch; Town Lattice; Long; Paddleford; Haupt; Warren; Pratt; Childs; Brown; Smith; Partridge; Post; McCallum; Suspension

An ingenious "pre-fabricated" girder recently made its appearance in Oregon. These are old railroad flatcars upon which one can construct a "covered bridge." At this news, some covered bridge purists grunt *harumph*! Others claim this is re-cycling of the very best kind.

Presently, there are three known examples of flatcars used in this manner:

China Ditch - Gilliam County
Dave Britch - Douglas County
Warner Canyon - Lake County

It is only a matter of time before more will appear. □

Why Are Bridges Covered

While some romanticists want to believe that bridges were covered for the sake of art, or kissing a pretty girl while inside the bridge, or to be the subjects of poetry, there were pragmatic reasons also.

Farmers often headed for the nearby covered bridge to wait out a thunderstorm. Hobos slept in them regularly. At the Ritner Covered Bridge in Polk County, a number of residents installed their rural mail boxes in the bridge.

Bridges in Oregon were built of wood – a locally available renewable product. Wood was plentiful.

Huge trees stand for many decades in the forests and withstand all kinds of weather but once the tree is cut, wood dries. When cut wood gets wet (rained on) it becomes vulnerable to rot.

It was determined by highway bridge engineers that a bridge built of wood might have a decade of life. But if the bridge had a cover, it might last three to five times longer.

Why are bridges covered? To keep the rain off.

This covered bridge, now long gone, was on a county road near Mitchell in Wheeler County. Although it seldom rains here, the covered design was available so one was built. The story goes that the large windows allowed the sharp winds to blow through the span without blowing it over. —Fred Kildow collection

Name: **Belknap** Lane County

Structure No. 39C123 *World Guide* No. 37-20-11

Type/year: Howe 1966 (1992)

Length: 120 feet

Spans: McKenzie River

Owner: Lane County

Nearest town: McKenzie Bridge

Nearest main highway: No. 126

STATUS	
OPEN TO:	
VEHICLES	☑
WALKERS	☑
BIKERS	☑
Status subject to change	

→From Interstate-5, Exit at Springfield. Take Highway No. 126 to the village of McKenzie Bridge then to McKenzie River Drive (about 36 miles). Proceed for about 1 mile to King Road West.

Named for early pioneers, Belknap Bridge is used for local traffic. It is also known as the "McKenzie River Bridge" It replaces three earlier covered bridges that were built in 1890, 1911 and 1938, the latter washed out in 1964. In 1975, the present bridge was modified by adding windows along its south side to let in light. This bridge, in the Deschutes National Forest, regularly gets a dusting of snow in winter. Recent rehabilitation to Belknap Covered Bridge included redecking the entire bridge, new rails, new roof, new siding, new white paint and workers pulled out encroaching trees and stumps. The bridge is now a beauty to photograph. □

Name: **Bohemian Hall** Linn County
Structure No. 12890 *World Guide* No. 37-22-07
Type/year: Howe 1947
Length: 120 feet
Spans: *moved*
Nearest town: Albany
Nearest Highway: Interstate-5

→ The various dismantled parts of this covered bridge are presently in Timber Linn Park about 1 mile east of the airport at Albany awaiting assembly.

This bridge once spanned Crabtree Creek, and was known as the Richardson Gap Bridge for many years, then renamed Bohemian Hall. In 1988, it was dismantled and stored. Our photograph (top) shows the bridge set up over Crabtree Creek. The lower picture is the skeleton while stored in a highway department maintenance yard.

The Albany Chamber of Commerce told the authors the present moving and reassembling project was being handled by the Albany JayCees and the Oregon Army National Guard. Apparently no schedule for completion of the work has been announced. □

—Bert Webber photo

Name: **Cascadia** Linn County

Structure No. 1356 *World Guide* No. 37-22-17

Type/Year: Howe 1928 (1994)

Length: 120 feet

Spans: South Santiam River

Owner: State of Oregon

Nearest town: Cascadia

Nearest main highway: No. 20

STATUS	
OPEN TO:	
VEHICLES	☑
WALKERS	☑
BIKERS	☑
Status subject to change	

→ From Interstate-5 take either Brownsville - Sweet Home Exit or Lebanon Exit. Proceed through Sweet Home, then drive 14 miles on Highway No. 20 to Cascadia. The bridge is on Cascadia State Park Road.

This is a unique, one-of-a-kind, on-deck wooden truss bridge. When the bridge became unsafe and was closed, the state wanted to replace it with a concrete span.

Fred Kildow, of the Covered Bridge Society of Oregon, wrote that it should be kept. He said "what a true gem we have in this bridge and I asked to preserve it in place." His letter, and others, was seen by the right people because a decision was made to rebuild it.

As this was the only bridge over the river for some distance, the U. S. Army Corps of Engineers installed a Bailey bridge over the top of the old bridge until repairs could be made. The work called for new trusses and a new deck. A state engineer said the shiny surfaces of the new glue-laminated wooden trusses were carefully, "roughed" to resemble the historical original trusses. The job was finished in 1994.

Looking at our picture, is this really a covered bridge? Where are the traditional side boards and a roof? The roadway is the roof!

Turn to Mott Memorial Covered Bridge and be surprised at some absorbing information about covered bridges ☐

Name: **Cavitt** Douglas County
Structure No. 19C18 *World Guide* No. 37-10-06
Type/year: Howe 1943
Length: 70 feet

STATUS	
OPEN TO:	
VEHICLES	☑
WALKERS	☑
BIKERS	☑
Status subject to change	

Spans: Little River at confluence with Cavitt Creek
Owner: Douglas County
Nearest town: Glide
Nearest main highway: No. 138

→Leave Interstate-5 at Roseburg Exit #124 then follow Highway No.
138, for 16 miles to Glide, turn right at Little River Road and proceed
south 8 miles to the bridge on the right..

Some of the covered bridges have windows along the sides
for illumination and this is one of them. But its unique and
photogenic Tudor style portals set Cavitt Creek bridge apart
from other Oregon covered bridges. It started out with a
plank deck but this is now asphalt covered. ☐

Name: **Cedar Crossing** Multnomah County   Fred Kildow collection
World Guide No. 37-26-X2
Type/year: Deck Girder (Glulam stringer) 1982
Length: 60 ft 1 span
Spans: Johnson Creek Owner: Multnomah County
Nearest town: Within City of Portland at 134th St. SE
              and Deardorf Road

STATUS	
OPEN TO:	
VEHICLES	☑
WALKERS	☑
BIKERS	☑
Status subject to change	

→From the freeway (I-5), take Foster Road Exit East to 134th Street then south to sharp turn to the east and down very steep, narrow grade on Deardorf Road into the gully.

While the purists call this merely a "roofed span," the local folks just call it "our covered bridge." To see the old, relic, narrow, open span here for many years give way to the new covered bridge, gave neighbors something to be proud of. The bridge is on a tight U-turn at the bottom of a gully in which flows often flooding Johnson Creek. The older open span, built in the days of Model T Fords was too narrow for today's vehicles therefore it had to be replaced.

If the picturesque vicinity could have spoken, it would have pleaded for a covered bridge rather than a span of Spartan pre-stressed concrete.

Some influential people wanted to dress up the neighborhood, so a covered bridge was built. The bridge's inside is finished in knotty-pine. The interior is brightly lighted at night. As this bridge is the only crossing of Johnson Creek for quite a distance, pedestrians are protected from speeding cars by a wide path separated from the roadway, but still within the bridge by a stout guard rail. For pictures, one will need to park at a safe place then walk back. □

Name: **Centennial** Lane County

World Guide No. 37-20-41

Type/year: Howe 1987

Length: 84 ft

Spans: Coast Fork Willamette River

STATUS
OPEN TO:
WALKERS ☑
BIKERS ☑
Status subject to change

Nearest town: Within City of Cottage Grove

Nearest main highway: Interstate-5

→From the I-5 freeway, take Cottage Grove Exit then proceed on Highway No. 99 into town. Make right turn on Main Street. Wander thorough the delightful town for 5 blocks until you see the bridge on the right.

The uniqueness of this covered bridge is that it is built from some of the remains of two others, the Meadows which was near Mapleton, and the Brumbaugh near Cottage Grove. This project was part of the Centennial celebration of the city. Centennial Walking Bridge, as it is often called, is a 3/8-inch scale of the Chambers Covered Bridge just a few blocks to the south.

Centennial Covered Bridge is on Main Street, on the west side of the original downtown area. The interior is lighted. In summer, all of the window boxes are ablaze with colorful flowers. The bridge can be a challenge for which to find good camera angles. □

Name: **Chambers** Lane County
World Guide No. 37-20-40
Type/year: Howe 1925
Length: 78 ft
Spans: Coast Fork Willamette River
Owner: Private
Nearest town: Is within City of Cottage Grove.
Nearest main highway: Interstate-5

STATUS:
CLOSED ☑
Status subject to change

Chambers Bridge as viewed from the east portal. (Inset) Shear weight of the bridge is causing it to crunch itself.

→From the I-5 freeway, take Cottage Grove Exit then proceed on Highway No. 99 into town. Make right turn on Main Street. Drive through the delightful town for 5 blocks until you see Centennial Covered Bridge on the right. At the corner, make left turn into South River Road and drive south a few blocks – about 3/4 of a mile – to Tyler Street. Bridge is on the left.

This former railroad bridge ran to the Frank Chambers Mill in town. Chambers Covered Bridge is a very tall bridge to accommodate high-loaded logging trains. It was an engineering accomplishment to design the trusses at a very high angle then add triple tension rods in order to support the very heavily loaded trains. Use of the bridge ceased after the mill burned in 1943. This is the only covered bridge of its type and the only covered railroad bridge standing in Oregon.

Although this bridge is beginning to sag, and is dangerous to climb on, it is photogenic because of its unique shape. ☐

Name: **China Ditch**   Gilliam County
World Guide No.: 37-11-X1
Type/Year: Railroad flatcar 1990
Length: 67 feet
Spans: China Ditch
Owner: City of Arlington
Nearest Town: Within City of Arlington.
Nearest main highway: Interstate-84

STATUS	
OPEN TO:	
WALKERS	☑
BIKERS	☑
Status subject to change	

→Take Arlington Exit off the freeway (I-84) or, if one can't pull off for a rest stop, slow down and view the covered bridge from the right side of the east-bound lane.

China Ditch is a spring run-off drain from the hills behind Arlington, which is nestled at the mouth of Alkali Canyon on the Columbia River. The ditch, running through the middle of town, was an impediment to the potential beauty of the site so a number of businessmen decided that a covered bridge over the concrete-lined ditch would be an esthetic improvement. Steve Seed, of the Chemical Waste Management Company, one of the firms, was the site manager.

For a solid deck, they bought an 85-foot long railroad flatcar. This was cut to 67-feet to appropriately fit the ditch. This was a community-wide project. The property (Earl Snell Memorial Park), and the new bridge, are owned by the city. The bridge (inside) is 8-ft. 2-in. wide. It can accommodate vehicles, if some emergency came up and this was required, but the intent is for a "people-walking bridge."

> Some covered bridge purists shudder at this bridge because it does not have "trusses" and other accouterments of the historical covered bridge. Nevertheless, the bridge gets countless numbers of visitors every year. This is because, in the first place, it is a "covered bridge." This bridge is "different." It's easily accessible. Folks love to look at it and walk through it. Arlington is also a nice place along the freeway to take a rest.

The Big River Band Festival Committee maintains the bridge. There is a major school brass band festival and concert in the park each June. □

Bridge Weight Limits

From time to time, particularly in the past, when a covered bridge has been damaged or is just plain deteriorated from old age, bridge inspectors impose weight limits on given bridges.

2 TON WEIGHT LIMIT
(1 ton = 2,000 pounds)

has been imposed several times. Can the public visualize what "2 tons" is?
Here are some current examples.

1995 Model Vehicles:	Curb Weight*
Toyota Land Cruiser	4,760 over weight
Cadallic Fleetwood	4,500 over weight
Chev. Caprice Wagon	4,473 over weight
Chev. Caprice Classic	4,061 over weight
Lincoln Towncar	4,031 over weight
Jeep Cherokee Wagon	3,900
Mercury Villager/Nissan Quest	3,870
Plymouth Grand Caravan	3,800
Plymouth Caravan	3,400
Ford Taurus Sedan	3,104
Saturn SW-2 Wagon	2,477
Honda Civic Hatchback	2,250

*Empty. Add weight of each passenger, gasoline, full-size spare wheel/tire, groceries, lunch, etc.
Sources: Interviews with new car dealers February 1995

Name: **Chitwood** Lincoln County

Structure No. 42C09 *World Guide* No. 37-21-03

Type/year: Howe 1926 (Rebuilt 1984)

Length: 96 feet

Spans: Yaquina River

Owner: Lincoln County

Nearest town: Eddyville

Nearest main highway: No. 20

STATUS	
OPEN TO:	
VEHICLES	☑
WALKERS	☑
BIKERS	☑
Status subject to change	

→From Interstate-5 use Corvallis/Lebanon Exit and turn west on Highway No. 20 passing through Corvallis and Philomath. About milepost 17, watch closely on left, as the bridge is just a few feet from the highway and it is easy to speed by it.

Citizens decided that their beloved but dilapidated Chitwood Covered Bridge needed to be rebuilt otherwise it might be demolished. Partly through the efforts of the Oregon Covered Bridge Society, and others, it was restored to the tune of $244,000. Some funds were from a federally financed rehabilitation program. In 1984, the work was completed.

Chitwood goes way back in Oregon history. It had a general store, post office (1887-1945) and was a station on the railroad. This covered bridge is painted dark red. □

Name: **Coyote Creek** Lane County

Structure No. 39C409 *World Guide* No. 37-20-02

Type/year: Howe 1922

Length: 60 feet

Spans: Coyote Creek

Owner: Lane County

Nearest town: Hadleyville

Nearest main highway: No. 126

STATUS	
OPEN TO:	
VEHICLES	☑
WALKERS	☑
BIKERS	☑
Status subject to change	

→From Interstate-5, take Exit No. 194 north of Eugene into I-105 westbound. In town, turn right on 11th Street (Highway No. 126) and go to Veneta then go south about 6½ miles on Territorial Highway. Next turn west for 1 mile on Battle Creek Road.

This bridge, on the route of the original 1851 Territorial Road, had many names including "Battle Creek Bridge" and "Swing Log Bridge." After the roof collapsed from 3 feet of snow in 1970 – the locals called it "unusual weather" – the roof was replaced. Coyote Covered Bridge is closed to trucks, but cars use it every day. □

Name: **Crawfordsville** Linn County
Structure No. 12819 *World Guide* No. 37-20-15
Type/year: Howe 1932
Length: 105 feet
Spans: Calapooia River
Owner: Linn County
Nearest town: Crawfordsville
Nearest main highway: No. 228

STATUS	
OPEN TO:	
VEHICLES	☑
WALKERS	☑
BIKERS	☑
Status subject to change	

→Use Exit #216 (Highway No. 228) from I-5 freeway and go east through Brownsville then to Crawfordsville.

This antique covered bridge once had rounded portals until modified for higher truck loads. In 1963, the bridge was bypassed when the highway was redesigned. The good condition of the bridge attests to the several major past renovation efforts.

Back in 1976, when a movie, *The Flood,* was made there, the bridge was repainted. Ten years later, volunteers from the Covered Bridge Society of Oregon did a major cleanup of over-grown weeds and brush. In 1987, funds ($23,000), were provided by a Community Services Consortium through a federal program for hiring unemployed persons to work on general renovation. In February 1966 the bridge was damaged in a flood but the bridge was repaired during summer 1997. ◇

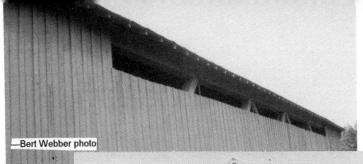
—Bert Webber photo

—John Snook photo

Name: **Currin**   Lane County

Structure No. 39C242   *World Guide* No. 37-20-22

Type/year: Howe 1925

Length: 105 feet

Spans: Row River

Owner: Lane County

Nearest town: Cottage Grove

Nearest main highway: Interstate-5

STATUS
OPEN TO:
WALKERS ☑
BIKERS ☑
Status subject to change

→From the freeway (I-5) take Cottage Grove Exit then take Row River Road out the southeast end of Cottage Grove about 2½ miles to Layng Road then drive about 1½ miles to the bridge. Note: By staying on Layng Road for 1 mile, see Mosby Creek Covered Bridge.

The original Currin Covered Bridge was here in 1883 then replaced with the present structure in 1925. But this was bypassed in favor of a modern concrete span parallel to it in 1979. Walkers can get on to the bridge, from the side away from the former approach, on Row River Road. Currin Covered Bridge underwent major rehabilitation in late 1995.

31

Name: **Dahlenburg** Linn County
World Guide No. 37-22-X1
Type/year: Howe 1989
Length: 20 feet
Spans: Ames Creek
Owner: City of Sweet Home
Nearest town: Within City of Sweet Home
Nearest main highway: Highway No. 20

STATUS	
OPEN TO:	
WALKERS	☑
BIKERS	☑
Status subject to change	

→Leave Interstate-5 at Albany Exit then take Highway No. 20 to Sweet Home. The bridge is in Sankey Park in the City of Sweet Home.

Dahlenburg Covered Bridge was named in honor of teacher Ben Dahlenburg, Sweet Home High School, whose Building Trades class designed and built the bridge as a class project. For their work, each student received a Report Card grade and a community "thank you."

The on-the-job training class wanted to build a house but suitable property was not available so, they decided to build a covered bridge. Following a model on exhibit in the public library, and after consulting some library books about covered bridges, the members of the class designed a bridge then scaled it in chalk on the floor of the school's shop. From this, a blueprint was developed then, with $2,000 city funds, the boys built the bridge.

This is a Howe truss bridge with the heaviest timbers being 4 x 8-inch and 4 x 6-inch. The 20-foot bridge is 12-feet wide. It is mounted across Ames Creek near Weddle Bridge, which this class also substantially rebuilt. The Dahlenberg Covered Bridge is intended just for pedestrians and bicyclists.

An additional covered bridge, a "portable" bridge, was built by the class then mounted on a donated mobile home chassis. This bridge is 8-feet wide and 20-feet long. The purpose of the trailer is to promote covered bridge preservation by being seen in parades and civic events of nearby communities.

One day, when the trailer-bridge was on exhibit in Sankey Park in Sweet Home, a man from New England, an area noted for a number of historic covered bridges, spied the little portable bridge and learned it had been built as a class project by the Building Trades class in the high school. He declared he'd like to buy it. He was told the price. Some days later, a check arrived with a note advising that some day he might come to pick it up but probably not. Indeed, this was a gentlemanly way of leaving a donation for a job well done.

The trailer-bridge did not have a permanent display place until 1993, when unique circumstances came together to bring a unique ending to this tale.

Turn to **Joel Whittemore** Covered Bridge in this book.

The students who built the Dahlenburg Covered bridge, worked on the Weddle Covered Bridge, and were involved with the construction of the trailer-bridge, were in the Building Trades Class of 1989. They were:

Ronald Care	Daniel Conn
Chad Logan	Chris Kennedy
Craig McKay	Brian Nicholson
Kevin Roll	Terry Seiber
David Stegal	Richard Totten

When all of the work was completed, the students decided to name their 20-foot bridge for their teacher, Ben Dahlenburg. □

Ends of many covered bridges were either totally knocked out, or badly damaged when high-loads of logs passed through the bridge.
—Bert Webber photo

Name: **Dave Birtch Dam**   Douglas County
World Guide No. 37-10-B
Type/year: Railroad flatcar   1981
Length: 22 feet
Spans: Willis Creek
Owner: Private
Nearest town: Dillard
Nearest main highway. No. 99

STATUS	
OPEN TO:	
VEHICLES	☑
WALKERS	☑
BIKERS	☑
Status subject to change	

→Leave Interstate-5 at Dillard Exit #112 or Round Prairie Exit #113. Proceed toward town. At Brockway Road, turn left and cross Umpqua River bridge. Proceed a few hundred feet to **Y**. Turn sharp left to Willis Creek Road and drive 4 miles. Bridge is on the left.

Dave Birtch always wanted a covered bridge. After he bought his acreage, be built his home on the crest of the hill then developed his land into a cattle, horse and sheep ranch. His private bridge is one-of-a-kind.

The Dave Birtch Dam Covered Bridge is almost square and from the road, at first sight, it looks like a flat-roofed house. It is just 22 feet long and 18-feet wide. The deck is a railroad flatcar cut in half each piece mounted side-by-side – the only such deck arrangement so far seen. The bridge sits atop a dam in Willis Creek, has interior lights and a wrought iron lockable gate. Due to usually dry conditions in summer, the winch in the south window lowers and raises a 9-feet high, 16-feet wide steel gate to seasonally dam the creek for water storage in a 100 yard long reservoir. This is for cattle and a fire department when needed. Find some limited turn-around space for cars across the dam. Best camera time is on a summer afternoon. ☐

Name: **Deadwood** Lane County

Structure No. 16-9W-25 *World Guide* No. 37-20-38

Type/year: Howe 1932   (1986)

Length: 105 feet

Spans: Deadwood Creek

Owner: Lane County

STATUS
OPEN TO:
VEHICLES ☑
WALKERS ☑
BIKERS ☑
Status subject to change

Nearest town: Alpha (site) and Deadwood

Nearest main highway: Highway No. 36

→Deadwood Covered Bridge is on Highway 36, the direct 34-mile scenic route between Junction City (Highway No. 99E / 99W) and Florence. After 44 miles, take Deadwood Creek Road northbound for 5 miles to Deadwood Loop. The bridge is about 1/4-mile.

→Or, from Interstate-5, take Exit No. 194 north of Eugene, into I-105 Bypass westbound. In town, turn right on 11th Street (Highway No. 126) and go to Mapleton. Turn right to Highway No. 36 by way of Swisshome to Deadwood then about 5 miles to Deadwood Loop Road to bridge.

Our photograph shows the bridge during the early days of its operation. For some time the bridge was closed to vehicles, but it was rebuilt and rededicated in 1986 and presently handles automobiles and light trucks up to only 5 tons. (A concrete span about 1/2-a-mile away takes the heavy traffic.) Deadwood Covered Bridge, with one portal at a curve in the road, has a special banked deck – a "tilt" – so, in wet weather, vehicles have less tendency to slip. ☐

35

—Bert Webber photo

Name: **Dorena** Lane County
Structure No. 21-2W-24A *World Guide* No. 37-20-23
Type/year: Howe 1949
Length: 105 feet
Spans: Row River
Owner: Lane County
Nearest town: Dorena
Nearest main highway: Interstate-5

STATUS
OPEN TO:
WALKERS ☑
BIKERS ☑
Status subject to change

→Take Cottage Grove Exit from the freeway (I-5), then follow Mosby Creek Road to Garoutte Road. Go about 2½ miles to Shoreview Road making a right turn. Proceed southeast about 6½ miles to the bridge.

When Dorena Dam was constructed, the townsite, Dorena, was flooded by the rising water in the reservoir therefore everyone moved to the present site. Dorena Covered Bridge was bypassed in 1973 for a new concrete span, but the covered bridge received rehabilitation funds for partial work in 1987. For years, the bridge was known as "Star Bridge," named for a large private ranch on which there was a post office (1891 - 1923). Dorena Covered Bridge was rebuilt in 1996 which included windows to allow more light and better air flow. When re-opened, visitors found the bridge had a Highway Safety Rest Area next to it.◇

OLD DRIFT CREEK BRIDGE. NEW BRIDGE OVER BEAR CREEK SAME PLAN

Name: **Drift Creek** Lincoln County

→*Demolished and rebuilt on Bear Creek - Reopen summer 1999*

Structure No. 10803 *World Guide* No. 37-21-14

Type/year: Howe 1914   (Body rebuilt 1999)

Length: 66 feet 10 inches

Spans: Bear Creek

STATUS
OPEN TO:
WALKERS ☑
Status subject to change

Owner: Bridge concrete base private. Bridge house Lincoln County

Nearest town: Rose Lodge

Nearest main highway: No. 18

→Take Highway 22 from Salem which runs into Hwy 18. Proceed on Hwy 18 to Rose Lodge Store and Fire Station then continue to next road (Bear Rd) turn left and go up hill for 9/10th mile. See Red bridge on left in gully at 1111 Bear Road. 10-car parking lot on the left. If you pass MP 1, you have gone too far.

"This bridge belonged to the people of Lincoln County and I could not stand to see it demolished," said Laura Sweitz. By agreement with the county, which owned the old bridge, Kerry and Laura Sweitz were given salvage rights in exchange for rebuilding it, maintaining it and providing public access on a piece of their property on Bear Creek. The house portion of bridge is under county ownership. "This is a positive thinking project where everybody helps," said Laura who formed a non-profit corporation "Save the Covered Bridges, Inc." through which a formal engineering study was donated, and materials needed for rebuilding the span were accepted as only about half the old bridge's remains were usable. The bridge is as a memorial to the pioneers. The concrete base for the bridge was built to Oregon Department of Transportation standards so Kerry Sweitz's heavy equipment can safely use it. As there is no room beyond the bridge for a turn-around, and the private residence is just a few feet from the far end of the bridge where children play, visitors are invited to park in the spaces on the road and walk 30 feet to the bridge. ◇

37

See the picture on page 17
—Bert Webber photos

Name: **Eagle Point** Jackson County
Structure No. 29C202 *World Guide* No. 37-15-02
Type/year: Queenpost 1922
Length: 58 feet
Spans: Little Butte Creek
Owner: City of Eagle Point
Nearest town: Within City of Eagle Point
Nearest main highway: No. 62

STATUS	
OPEN TO:	
WALKERS	☑
BIKERS	☑
Status subject to change	

→Leave freeway (I-5) at Central Point Exit (#32) then proceed east over the freeway for about 1 mile to signal. Turn left on Table Rock Road and go north 1 mile to signal. Turn right on Vilas Road and drive east to signal. Turn left onto Highway No. 62 then drive north through White City community to City of Eagle Point. The bridge is seen at Main Street and Royal Avenue.

Historically called "Antelope Creek Covered Bridge," this bridge was removed from Antelope Creek in 1987, then reinstalled, by community-wide effort, over Little Butte Creek in town. The bake sales, raffles and other money-making events, brought in $75,000 in cash, materials and labor for the project.

As originally built, the bridge had solid sides but for use in town, where natural light was needed inside the structure, arched windows were cut into it. The bridge is for pedestrians only and is illuminated with flourescent lights. It is used mostly by children who attend a school one block away. This is probably the only covered bridge in Oregon equipped with a fire sprinkler system. As seen in our pictures, it is parallel to the concrete bridge for motor vehicles. ☐

Name: **Earnest** Lane County
Structure No. 39C176 *World Guide* No. 37-20-35
Type/year: Howe 1903 (replaced in 1938) (1990)
Length: 75 feet
Spans: Mohawk River
Owner: Lane County
Nearest town: Marcola
Nearest main highway: Interstate-5

STATUS	
OPEN TO:	
VEHICLES	☑
WALKERS	☑
BIKERS	☑
Status subject to change	

→Leave the freeway (I-5) at Springfield Exit taking I-105 and proceed east through town to 42nd Street and turn north to Marcola Road then eastward about 14 miles through Marcola to Pachelka Road to the bridge.

This covered bridge was known as the Adams Avenue Bridge (1903-1938) then as the Mohawk River Bridge and as the Paschelke Bridge. The present span was the feature in a Civil War era movie *Shenendoah*. When the studio finished its work in 1987, the bridge was repainted. In 1990, there was rehabilitation work here. As this bridge sits on piers above the river, and there are no obstructions nearby, and recently much brush and trees were removed, photography is now better than usual. ◇

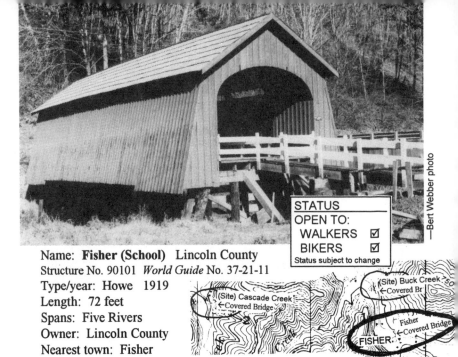

—Bert Webber photo

Name: **Fisher (School)** Lincoln County
Structure No. 90101 *World Guide* No. 37-21-11
Type/year: Howe 1919
Length: 72 feet
Spans: Five Rivers
Owner: Lincoln County
Nearest town: Fisher
Nearest main highway: No. 34

→Probably the better way to get to Fisher Covered Bridge is from Corvallis on Highway 34. (Corvallis is about 10 miles west of Interstate-5.) Pass Alsea then 20 more scenic (winding), miles to Forest Service Road No. 141. This road is marked:

FIVE RIVERS - FISHER ROAD.

Keep going about 1 mile past Buck Creek Road to the bridge. (On our map, note two sites where earlier covered bridges were located.) Road No. 141 eventually comes out at Deadwood Covered Bridge. While there is another forest road (No. 1560) to Fisher from Yachats on the coast, the authors do not recommend it.

Fisher Covered Bridge was built in 1919 with major repairs in 1927. The once thriving village had a post office (1892-1911) then again from 1912 until 1942. The Fisher Elementary School nearby causes many folks to call the bridge the "Fisher School Bridge."

Because of old age, this covered bridge has been bypassed with a concrete span therefore the covered bridge mainly serves hikers and school kids. In 1998 the bridge was suggested for demolition but applications for grants for its repair are being considered.

This is rugged, isolated, low elevation forest country. The river, "Five Rivers River," is the name given to the larger stream flowing from the confluence of five creeks: Alder, Buck, Cherry, Cougar, Crab. The river itself is a tributary of Alsea River.

For more details of this forested and multi-creek area, refer to TIDEWATER, OREG. TOPOGRAPHIC MAP. ◇

Fred Kildow collection

Name: **Fourtner** Polk County
World Guide No. 37-27-03
Type/year: Queenpost 1932
Length: 66 feet
Spans: South Yamhill River
Owner: Private
Nearest town: Grande Ronde
Nearest main highway: No. 18

STATUS:
CLOSED   ☑
Status subject to change

→From Interstate-5 at Salem, take Highway No. 22 through the city following markers for OCEAN BEACH. At Valley Junction, continue westerly on Highway No. 18 to Grande Ronde. Make a right turn on Grande Ronde Road and go to 688A Ackerson Road. Go left for 1 block then take left side of Y junction into yard at the house. This is Private Property. Seek permission before going forward to the bridge.

This private boxed span is also known as the Alva "Doc" Fourtner Covered Bridge. Doc and his wife, Lydia, maintained dairy cows and installed the bridge for the purpose of keeping their herd dry while moving them between fields back-and-forth across the river.

The bridge was a very long job to construct, having been built with hand tools. It was not intended for motor vehicles. One end of the bridge is now barricaded, but there is a small door for walkers. □

Name: **Gallon House** Marion County

Structure No. 5381 *World Guide* No. 37-24-01

Type/year: Howe 1915

—John Snook photo

Length: 84 feet

Spans: Abiqua Creek

Owner: Marion County

Nearest town: Silverton

Nearest main highway: No. 214

STATUS	
OPEN TO:	
VEHICLES	☑
WALKERS	☑
BIKERS	☑
Status subject to change	

→From the freeway(I-5) take Salem Market Street Exit to Lancaster Drive N.E. then turn left watching for road signs for Silverton. Turn right on Silverton Road then, in town, take Highway No. 214 northbound, about half-a-mile to Hobart Road. Turn west for another half mile to the bridge.

This covered bridge is made of timber from top to bottom, including the pilings it rests on: shake roof, wood siding and deck, wood approach and ramps.

> Gallon House Covered Bridge appears to have been named because it was a way-point for running liquor from Mt. Angel, a "wet" town, to folks in Silverton, a "dry" town before prohibition.

The destructive 1964 flood at Christmas, caused quite a bit of damage but the county fixed it because of historical interest. The results of this work lasted 20 more years when, in 1985, a chord was damaged therefore closing the bridge. Although the structure was, by principle, over-age and some wanted to get rid of it, workers fixed it, painted it, placed a 10 TON LIMIT sign on it, then reopened it to traffic.

Gallon House Covered Bridge is the only covered bridge in Oregon with hinged portals – like a transom that can be raised and lowered by drivers of very tall trucks.

With continuing maintenance, this historical covered bridge should continue to offer nostalgia to everyone who wishes to drive through it. □

42

—Bert Webber photo

Name: **Gilkey** Linn County
Structure No. 12943 *World Guide* No. 37-22-04
Type/year: Howe 1939
Length: 120 feet
Spans: Thomas Creek
Owner: Marion County
Nearest town: Scio
Nearest main highway: Interstate-5

STATUS	
OPEN TO:	
VEHICLES	☑
WALKERS	☑
BIKERS	☑
Status subject to change	

→From the freeway (I-5), use Jefferson Exit and drive toward Scio but turn southeast at Robinson Road and proceed southerly to the bridge. There is limited off-road parking near a pump house.

The community of Gilkey is presumed to have been around a train station, probably on the Oregon Electric Railway. Such a place is not on the Southern Pacific Railroad Trackside Stations Map, neither is it listed in *Oregon Geographic Names* nor in Helbock's *Oregon Post Offices 1847-1982*.

Where the span crosses Thomas Creek, the waterway more resembles a river due to its width. There are many fishing holes and the swimming has never diminished through the ages. Gilkey Covered Bridge is a general-use structure and is regularly maintained. In 1987 it was painted, experienced deck reinforcing and other significant work. In 1998, it was substantially rebuilt. ◇

Name: **Goodpasture** Lane County
Structure No. 39C118 *World Guide* No. 37-20-10
Type/year: Howe 1938   (1986)
Length: 165 feet
Spans: McKenzie River
Owner: Lane County
Nearest town: Vida
Nearest main highway: No. 126

STATUS	
OPEN TO:	
VEHICLES	☑
WALKERS	☑
BIKERS	☑
Status subject to change	

→Leave Interstate-5 at Springfield Exit then proceed through the city and eastward on Highway 126, about 25 miles, to the bridge which is on the western outskirts of Vida.

At the present time, this is the second longest covered bridge standing in Oregon. Because of it's attractive line of louvered windows, which breaks up the otherwise solid white sides, this bridge is one of the most photogenic. (It's also easy to get to.) Goodpasture Covered bridge was substantially rebuilt in 1986 and when finished could once again handle loaded log trucks. ☐

Name: **Grave Creek** Josephine County
—Bert Webber photo

Structure No. 141005 *World Guide* No. 37-17-01

Type/year: Howe   1920

Length: 105 feet

Spans: Grave Creek

Owner: Josephine County

Nearest town: Sunny Valley

Nearest main highway: Interstate-5

STATUS		Temporarily Closed See text
OPEN TO:		
VEHICLES	☑	
WALKERS	☑	
BIKERS	☑	
Status subject to change		

→From freeway (I-5), use Sunny Valley Exit at the bottom of a steep draw. This is about 15 miles north of Grants Pass. The covered bridge can be seen from the freeway. Follow the old highway to the bridge.

The locality and community had several earlier names, but Sunny Valley was adopted in 1954. Its post office lasted until 1965 when the mail was transferred to a rural route. Josephine County had a number of covered bridges in its glorious past but these dwindled to just this one until two new bridges were recently built. (See Tissot Memorial at Wolf Creek and Wayne A. Perry at Williams.)

When the freeway was built in the 1960's, Grave Creek Covered Bridge, on Highway No. 99, was bypassed by about 1/2 mile. Although Grave Creek Covered Bridge had some maintenance and new paint, its condition deteriorated in the following years because of shortage of funds. At this writing (Mar. 1999) the bridge is closed for structural repairs and is expected to be reopened in about one year. ◇

45

Name: **Hannah** Linn County
Structure No. 12948 *World Guide* No. 37-22-02
Type/year: Howe 1936
Length: 105 feet
Spans: Thomas Creek
Owner: Linn County
Nearest town: Jordan
Nearest main highway: No. 226

STATUS	
OPEN TO:	
VEHICLES	☑
WALKERS	☑
BIKERS	☑
Status subject to change	

→From Interstate-5, use the Jefferson Exit and go toward Scio then Highway 226 to Burmester Creek Road.

Greatly photogenic, Hannah Covered Bridge, light and airy, because of its wide-open sides, is recognizable in a number of TV commercials. Accordingly, it is well-kept which includes timely use of fresh paint. It is a handy diving platform for summer swimmers during steamy Willamette Valley summers. □

—Bert Webber photo

Name: Harris Benton County

Structure No. 1441 *World Guide* No. 37-02-04

Type/year: Howe 1929-? (1936)

Length: 75 feet

Spans: Marys River

Owner: Benton County

Nearest town: Wren

Nearest main highway: No. 20

STATUS	
OPEN TO:	
VEHICLES	☑
WALKERS	☑
BIKERS	☑
Status subject to change	

→From the Corvallis/Lebanon Exit in the freeway (I-5), proceed to the west past Corvallis, Philomath to Wren. Watch for small direction signs to the bridge.

For years, this structure was called the Marys River Bridge. Although it was and is at the Harris community, the post office was named Elam to avoid confusion with a Linn County town, Harrisburg. Although county records indicate 1936 as the building date, various old timer neighbors vigorously disagree declaring about 1929 was more likely. The sweeping curves at the bridge do not deter fast drivers which can be hazardous to visiting picture makers. □

Name: **Hayden** Benton County
Structure No. 14538 *World Guide* No. 37-02-05
Type/year: Howe   1918
Length: 91 feet
Spans: Alsea River
Owner: Benton County
Nearest town: Alsea
Nearest main highway: No. 34

STATUS	
OPEN TO:	
VEHICLES	☑
WALKERS	☑
BIKERS	☑
Status subject to change	

→Leave Interstate-5 at the Corvallis/Lebanon Exit then follow Highway No. 20 west through Corvallis to junction with Highway No. 34 in Philomath, which take –its a twist-and-turn but pretty drive – to Alsea. Then look for Hayden Road. Take it a short way to the bridge.

Hayden Covered Bridge appears to be a little "squat" due to its non-perpendicular sides as though it was braced for the winds that sometimes roar though its locale. Actually, the sloping sides protect the buttress supports from lots of rain that falls here. Usually, these supports are outside of the walls. See these on several covered bridges including the new Wayne A. Perry Covered Bridge. ☐

Name: **Hoffman** Linn County
Structure No. 1724 *World Guide* No. 37-22-08
Type/year: Howe 1936
Length: 90 feet
Spans: Crabtree Creek
Owner: Linn County
Nearest town: Crabtree
Nearest main highway: No. 20

STATUS	
OPEN TO:	
VEHICLES	☑
WALKERS	☑
BIKERS	☑
Status subject to change	

→Leave freeway (I-5) at Albany Exit taking Highway 20 eastward to village of Crabtree, then north on Hungry Hill Road to the bridge – about 1 mile.

A uniqueness of this bridge is the "bumper" on the up-river side to deflect floating debris in spring floods. Some years back, the portals were redesigned, from original round-top openings, to permit large trucks with high loads to safely pass through it. It is an attractive bridge with unique gothic style windows.

> During severe thunder storms, if traffic is light, a momentary stop in the bridge with the car windows open, one can listen to rain pounding on the tin roof. It has been suggested this sound might be like being inside a snare drum during a Sousa March.

Hoffman Covered bridge is in continual use. ☐

Name: **Horse Creek** Douglas County

Structure No. 16-5E-24 *World Guide* No. 37-10-14

Type/year: Howe   1930 (moved to Myrtle Creek, rebuilt 1990-92)

Length: 105 feet

Spans: Myrtle Creek (x Horse Creek)

Owner: City of Myrtle Creek

Nearest town: Within the City of Myrtle Creek

Nearest main highway: Interstate-5

→From the freeway (I-5), take the very slow-speed Myrtle Creek Exit then proceed down hill and through the town. Near the bottom of the hill, at 1st Street, make right turn for public parking lot. Or, stay on the main street and go to the bottom of the hill, take the right fork and go a few hundred feet to the bridge slightly behind you on the right. Plenty of parking here then walk through the bridge to photograph it from the opposite end.

Sometimes keeping track of covered bridges that have popular names long associated with a former location, can be confusing. Known for decades as "Horse Creek Covered Bridge" this structure was dismantled and by community effort was hauled to Mill Site Park in Myrtle Creek. After a period of frustration, the bridge was finally completed and opened for all to marvel over. ☐

Nostalgic view of Irish Bend Covered Bridge before being moved to Corvallis where it was rebuilt on the OSU campus.

Orville Erdman photo

Name: **Irish Bend** Benton County
World Guide No. 37-02-09
Type/year: Howe 1954 (moved to Corvallis rebuilt 1988)
Length: 60 feet
Spans: Oak Creek
Owner: State of Oregon
Nearest town: Within the campus of Oregon State University
Nearest main highway: No: 34

→Proceed from Interstate-5 using the Corvallis/Lebanon Exit, westbound, onto Highway No. 34. It's 10 miles to Corvallis. Go through town to the campus and ask at the Information kiosk for a map showing where the bridge is located and for parking instructions.

This historic bridge was first at a slough running more-or-less parallel with, but between the Willamette and Long Tom Rivers on Irish Bend Road near Monroe.

In 1988, the bridge was dismantled then moved to the Oregon State University campus. It presently serves bikers and walkers crossing Oak Creek on the campus. □

51

Name: **Joel Whittemore**   Linn County
World Guide No.: 37-22-20
Type/Year: Howe   1989
Length: 20 feet
Spans: Stone Brook Creek
Owner: City of Sweet Home
Nearest town: Within the City of Sweet Home
Nearest highway: No. 34

STATUS	
OPEN TO:	
WALKERS	☑
BIKERS	☑
Status subject to change	

→Leave Interstate-5 at Albany Exit then take Highway No. 20 to Sweet Home. Joel Whittemore Covered Bridge is in Clover Memorial Park in the City of Sweet Home.

Here is the little 8-feet wide and 20-feet long covered bridge that started its life on a trailer that was pulled in parades to promote covered bridge preservation. When not in use, it was parked between Dahlenburg and Weddle bridges in Sankey Park. This park was the only place where three covered bridges could be in a single snapshot.

We recall (*see* under Dahlenburg) that a man from the east bought the bridge then decided not to claim it for he believed it should remain in Sankey Park for all to enjoy. Fred Kildow, the dean of Oregon covered bridge "bridgers," wrote about what happened next in the Fall 1993 issue of *The Bridge Tender*:

> Early [in 1993], Don Menear, Sweet Home's park maintenance person and key figure in rebuilding Weddle Bridge, found that he had a need for a new foot bridge in Clover Memorial Park, located at the west entrance to Sweet Home. Joel Whittemore [the gentleman from New Hampshire who had purchased the trailer-bridge] was contacted and agreed to donate his covered bridge back to Sweet Home with one stipulation – the bridge bear his name when placed in the park. This pretty, white, twenty-foot Howe Truss covered bridge is a pleasing addition to Clover Memorial Park where it can be enjoyed by all. Thank you, Mr. Joel Whittemore for making this possible. □

Name: **Jordan** (Also known as "Stayton-Jordan") Marion County
Structure No. 12958 *World Guide* No. 37-24-02
Type/year: Howe 1937
  Moved to Pioneer Park, Stayton in 1988. Burned, December 1994. Rebuilt 1998.
Length: 90 feet
Spans: Santiam Canal-Salem Power Canal
Owner: City of Stayton
Nearest town: Within the City of Stayton
Nearest main highway: No: 22

STATUS
OPEN TO:
WALKERS ☑
BIKERS ☑
Status subject to change

→From the freeway (I-5) at Salem, take Highway No. 22 southeast to the Stayton-Sublimity crossroads. Turn right into Stayton.

The bridge was named for the community of Jordan, which was named for the Jordan Valley in Israel, and spanned Thomas Creek. It was relocated to Stayton as an historical attraction. The Jordan Bridge Company, a covered bridge preservation company, supervised fund raising, and thousands of man-hours, before the bridge was ready for pedestrian traffic. A Marine band played on dedication day in 1988.

Additional pictures on next page

During the Christmas Season in 1994, (December 20) the bridge was accidentally destroyed by fire from defective wiring in a string of colored seasonal lights. After much delay, a new bridge was built at the site and dedicated in fall, 1998. <>

Jordan Covered Bridge in its original role (page 53) as a "working" bridge carrying highway traffic. Later, It was installed (this page) in Pioneer Park, Stayton, as an historical bridge open to pedestrians. All that was left (lower) after the December 1994 fire – Stayton Fire-fighters viewed the remains the next day. After some delay, then over a period of many months, the bridge was rebuilt and completed in fall of 1998.

Name: **Lake Creek** Lane County
Structure No.: 39C386 *World Guide* No. 37-20-06

Type/year: Howe 1928
Length: 105 feet
Spans: Lake Creek
Owner: Lane County
Nearest town: Greenleaf
Nearest main highway: No: 36

STATUS	
OPEN TO:	
VEHICLES	☑
WALKERS	☑
BIKERS	☑
Status subject to change	

→From Florence on the Coast Highway No. 101, take Highway No. 126 to Mapleton then Highway No. 36 to Deadwood. Then to Nelson Mountain Road to about mile post 17. The bridge is nearby.

→Or, take Interstate-5 Eugene Exit then follow northward on Highway 99 about 8 miles to Highway No. 36. Proceed westerly about 30 miles to Nelson Mountain Road. The bridge is about 1 mile on this road.

Lake Creek Covered Bridge was also known as Nelson Mountain Bridge – often called just "Nelson Bridge." In 1984, there was a major refit which might cause some covered bridge purists to cringe. The old deck was replaced by a concrete span on concrete end piers and center pier. These improvements increased the load limit on the bridge but the covered bridge is still a "one lane" bridge. The portals were enlarged to eliminate damage that high loads of logs often cause by crashing the end panels of the covered bridge. ☐

STATUS
OPEN TO:
VEHICLES ☑
WALKERS ☑
BIKERS ☑
Status subject to change

Name: **Larwood** Linn County
Structure No.: 12876 *World Guide* No. 37-22-06
Type/year: Howe 1939
Length: 105 feet
Spans: At confluence of Roaring River and Crabtree Creek
Owner: Linn County
Nearest town: Lacomb
Nearest highway: No: 226

→Leave Interstate-5 at Jeffeson Exit and drive toward Scio. Take Highway No. 226 eastbound about 3 miles to Richardson Gap Road then on Larwood Drive (Fish Hatchery County Road No. 648) go about 4 more miles to the bridge.

Two earlier covered bridges, only a few feet apart, crossed both the Roaring River and Crabtree Creek. It is adjacent to a roadside park. According to *Ripley's Believe It Or Not,* this is the only example where a river empties into a creek! Larwood had roof repair and new siding in 1997.◇

Name: **Lost Creek** Jackson County
Structure No.: 29C262   *World Guide No.* 37-15-03
Type/year: Queenpost 1919 (*ca* 1881)
Length: 39 feet
Spans: Lost Creek
Owner: Lake Creek Historical Society
Nearest town: Lake Creek
Nearest main highway: No: 140

STATUS	
OPEN TO:	
WALKERS	☑
BIKERS	☑
Status subject to change	

→Leave freeway (I-5) at Central Point Exit (#32) then proceed east for about 1 mile to Table Rock Road (signal.) Turn left, proceed 1 mile to Vilas Road (signal). Turn right and drive east to Highway No. 62 (signal). Turn left, drive north to signal marked for CRATER LAKE at junction with Highway 140. (If you want to see Eagle Point Covered Bridge, stay on Highway No. 62 to Eagle Point which see in this book). Turn right about 12 miles to Lake Creek junction. Veer right. See sign HISTORIC BRIDGE 4½ MI. Follow signs to bridge.

Although challenged many times in its claim as the shortest covered bridge on an Oregon public highway, it is indeed the shortest at only 39 feet long. While the Southern Oregon Historical Society in-

For a 22-feet long bridge, see the Dave Birtch Dam Covered Bridge

sists that this bridge was built in 1919, a neighbor and her mother, who have always lived within a stone's throw of

the bridge, contend the span was put up between 1874 and 1881.

Pictures best in summer mid-day due to shadows from hills and trees.

The bridge was nearly lost during the 1964 flood. When first photographed by Bert Webber in 1970, Lost Creek Covered bridge was

Lost Creek Covered Bridge in 1971
—Bert Webber photo

Lost Creek Covered Bridge in 1995
—Bert Webber photo

Southern Oregon Historical Society insists this bridge was built in 1919 but Lake Creek Historical Society maintains the bridge was built about 1881 and posted this plaque saying so.
—Bert Webber photo

very dilapidated and nearly concealed among spindly trees and weeds. In 1979, the span was closed to vehicles when a concrete span was completed near by. In May 1985, the folks of rural Lake Creek community, which included the bridge, decided to save the bridge. They did not want it to be trashed without notice as had happened to nearby Yankee Creek Covered Bridge.

Evidence of original construction being pre-1919, is a remark that workers in 1987 reinstalled new portals *"which had been removed in 1919 to allow log trucks to go through without destroying the cover."*
—Fred Kildow

In summer 1990, Lost Creek Covered Bridge was hoisted from its old pillars by a borrowed crane, then set aside so new concrete piers could be built. When returned to its place, major renovation was done. Trees were located on private land, felled, then hand-hewn to meet original specifications. Most of the work, and use of equipment, was donated. Of cash required, $35,000, about half came as a result of many fund-raising events spearheaded by Ralph E. Wehinger, D.C., an avid covered bridge enthusiast.

> Dr. Wehinger, a Chiropractor in Eagle Point, was also instrumental in the planning, moving and installation of the Antelope Creek Covered Bridge over Little Butte Creek in Eagle Point – *See* Eagle Point Covered Bridge – and he worked on the restoration of McKee Covered Bridge – *See* McKee Covered Bridge – over the Applegate River.

Other funds came from the Parks and Recreation Department and from state lottery funds.

Lost Creek Covered Bridge is open for bikers and walkers with motor vehicles taking the concrete span a few yards away. The bridge is maintained by the Lake Creek Historical Society with repairs, when needed, recommended by Jackson County bridge inspectors. □

Name: **Lowell** Lane County
Structure No.: 19-1W-23 *World Guide* No. 37-20-18
Type/year: Howe 1945
Length: 165 feet
Spans: Middle Fork Willamette River
Owner: Lane County
Nearest town: Lowell
Nearest main highway: No: 58

STATUS	
OPEN TO:	
WALKERS	☑
BIKERS	☑
Status subject to change	

→From Lowell, follow Lowell-Jasper Road about 1 mile toward Highway No. 58 passing the bridge.

The history of this site reveals there was a ferry, "The Hyland Ferry," here followed in 1907 with "The Hyland Ferry Bridge." It was covered. A trucking accident during World War II damaged the bridge's alignment but the bridge could not be rebuilt, due to shortage of materials, until after the war. Then the bridge was rebuilt but without its roof.

With an anticipated raised water level in 1953 on the completion of the Dexter Dam, the highway, along with the bridge, was raised 6 feet. This is the only covered bridge in Oregon to cross a reservoir. In 1981, another truck damage, this time with a dump truck where the driver had not dropped the bed back into position, rammed into the end of the bridge. Damage was severe. After repairs, the bridge served until the opening of the new concrete span adjacent caused it to be closed in 1981. □

Name: **McKee** Jackson County
Structure No. 29C471 *World Guide* No. 37-15-06
Type/year: Howe 1917   (1990) (1995)
Length: 122 feet
Spans: Applegate River
Owner: Jackson County
Nearest town: Ruch (pron: Roosh)
Nearest main highway: No: 238

STATUS	
OPEN TO:	
WALKERS	☑
BIKERS	☑
Status subject to change	

→For directions, please turn to Wayne A. Perry Covered Bridge as the start from Medford for the McKee and the Wayne A Perry Covered Bridges is the same.

This span is probably the highest elevation, 45-feet, above any stream in Oregon where covered bridges are located. McKee Covered Bridge is only 8 miles north of the California line and is the farthest south of all covered bridges in Oregon. It was also called the Applegate River Covered Bridge.

It opened for traffic in 1917 and served regular traffic of gold miners and logging trucks until 1956 when, due to deterioration, was closed in favor of a new concrete span a short distance away.

> McKee Covered Bridge, where relief horses were once stabled, served as a rest stop between the Blue Ledge Mine and Jacksonville.

Destined to be torn down, the people wanted to keep "their bridge" so the county, a lodge, and a grange, put up the bucks for a new roof. More time flitted by and the bridge, except for the new top, continued to weaken. The county commissioners let the folks in the Ruch area know that it would require much "public support" ($$$) to preserve the bridge.

The adjacent McKee Picnic Ground is supervised by the Star Ranger District of the Rogue River National Forest. The park includes an excellent swimming hole, good fishing and a rustic picnic shelter with an immense fireplace made of river rocks. This had been built as a Civilian Conservation Corps (CCC) project in the 1930's. People flock to the site all summer long taking advantage of this isolated and serene public park.

To keep "their bridge," the neighbors engaged in every kind of fund-raising project imaginable and the money flowed in. The work was done. In 1990 the rehabilitated bridge was dedicated and opened for walkers and bikers.

In 1994, it was determined that some "Oregon weather" was seeping into the bridge causing some deterioration. The local preservation committee undertook the responsibility for half of $48,600 needed, on a cooperative plan with the Oregon Covered Bridge Maintenance and Rehabilitation program to pay the other half.

In late January 1995, the bridge was closed for repairs. This included all new siding for both sides. The upstream side has windows that were leaking therefore the leaks were stopped as part of the re-siding. Both end portals were also replaced. The estimated time to make the repairs was 30 days. At this writing, the work is in progress and on schedule with a re-opening planned for early March. The bridge will continue to be just for "walkers and bikers." This covered bridge has been the centerpiece of pride in the McKee Bridge Community. □

An historic covered bridge is part of the design for this United States postage stamp. It was issued in 1952 marking the Centennial of Engineering.
—Stamps from Bert Webber collection

Name: **Milo Academy**   Douglas County
World Guide No. 37-10-X1
Type/year: Steel through plate girder   1962
Length: 100 feet
Spans: South Umpqua River
Owner: Private
Nearest town: Milo
Nearest main highway No. 227

STATUS	
OPEN TO:	
VEHICLES	☑
WALKERS	☑
BIKERS	☑
Status subject to change	

→From freeway (I-5) take the Canyonville - Days Creek Exit #98. Follow Highway No. 227 easterly to the bridge.

This privately owned and maintained steel bridge primarily serves the campus of a Seventh Day Adventist boarding school. Over the years there have been 3 covered bridges at this site, the earlier spans having been made of wood. The present structure, which causes covered bridge purists to shake their heads in dismay, is steel with walls and a roof that only loosely resemble its forebears. Our larger, earlier book, *Oregon Covered Bridges* (1991) has pictures of all three bridges. □

Name: **Mott Memorial** Douglas County
Structure No. 4712-000-0.1 *World Guide* No. 37-10-15
Type/Year: Timber Deck Arch 1936
Length: 135 feet
Spans: North Umpqua River
Owner: U. S. Forest Service
Nearest Town: Glide
Nearest main Highway: No. 138

STATUS	
OPEN TO:	
VEHICLES	☑
WALKERS	☑
BIKERS	☑
Status subject to change	

→Leave Interstate-5 at Roseburg and take Highway No. 138 to Glide, then about 21 miles further to Steamboat Inn, then about another 1/2-a-mile to junction. Take right fork and cross the concrete bridge. Mott Memorial Bridge can be seen, upstream, about 1/4-mile, on right side of highway. At the bridge, turn right and cross the river on the bridge to parking area at opposite end of the bridge on Steamboat Ranger Station Road. Mott Covered Bridge is wheelchair accessible on steel walkways on both sides of the bridge.

When is an uncovered bridge a covered bridge?

At a glance, few folks would call this a covered bridge because it does not fit the popular description of one – a barn with holes in each end – through which there is a road, the bridge mounted over a waterway. In this case, the North Umpqua River.

A number of bridges built with wood truss supports, particularly in the early days, did not have side boards – walls – or roofs. Some were closed in at later dates. On some early railroad

65

bridges, roofs were omitted to pre-handle the trouble with the roofs being burned off by hot flying sparks. In the case of Mott Memorial Bridge, the roadway is the roof !

As seen in the specifications, the span is 135 feet long, but with its approaches, this unique on-deck road bridge totals 237 feet long. This bridge, a very rare type, according to Fred Kildow, of the Covered Bridge Society of Oregon, who investigated it, is a "braced spandrel, three-hinged timber arch truss."

According to a spokesman for Oregon Department of Transportation, this bridge was constructed by members of the Civilian Conservation Corps stationed at Coos Bay, then moved and installed at the present site. This was in 1936.

Kildow had been studying the Mott and Cascadia on-deck bridges for some time. It was he who determined they should be officially recognized as meeting the specifications to be classed as "covered bridges." As a result of his research and his instigation, a further study was conducted by The National Society for the Preservation of Covered Bridges (Inc.).

The official determination that the Mott Memorial Covered Bridge was indeed qualified as "covered," was announced on March 7, 1992 when a *World Guide* number was assigned to it.* The explanation applies to this bridge and to Cascadia State Park Covered Bridge (*which see*):

a) both of the structures were worthy of preservation, b) both supported themselves by means of two types of trusses typically found in recognized covered bridges, c) both structures were in fact bridges which are covered.

...most bridges one thinks of when one says "covered," are just that, i. e., not only roofed, but sideboarded. Neither of [these] two specimens is sideboarded [but the roadway is the roof]. —David W. Wright, President, National Society for the Preservation of Covered Bridges

The Mott Memorial Covered Bridge remembers nationally recognized Major Mott, author and sportsman who once had a fishing camp near the bridge site. This bridge has been dedicated as an Oregon Historical Civil Engineering landmark by Oregon Section of the American Society of Civil Engineers. □

---

* Extracted from "Oregon Gains Two Covered Bridges" by Fred Kildow in *The Bridge Tender.*" Vol. 13. No. 4. Winter '92-'93 pp. 2-4.

Name: **Mosby Creek** Lane County
ODOT No. 39C241 *World Guide* 37-20-27
Type/year: Howe 1920 (1990)
Length: 90 feet
Spans: Mosby Creek
Owner: Lane County
Nearest town: Cottage Grove
Nearest main highway: No: 227

STATUS	
OPEN TO:	
VEHICLES	☑
WALKERS	☑
BIKERS	☑
Status subject to change	

→From Interstate-5, take Cottage Grove Exit then in town, proceed east on Main Street (becomes Mosby Creek Road) to Layng Road. The bridge is just a stone's throw away.

This is Lane County's oldest covered bridge but with continuing maintenance, has continued to serve well. It was repainted in 1987. But the condition of the bridge was deteriorating in recent years so extensive work was done on this single-lane bridge in 1990. ☐

—Bert Webber photo

Name: **Neal Lane** Douglas County
Structure No. 10C220 *World Guide* 37-10-07
Type/year: Kingpost 1929-? (rebuilt 1939)
Length: 42 feet
Spans: Myrtle Creek
Owner: Douglas County
Nearest town: Myrtle Creek
Nearest main highway: Interstate-5

STATUS	
OPEN TO:	
VEHICLES	☑
WALKERS	☑
BIKERS	☑
Status subject to change	

→Leave freeway (I-5) at Myrtle Creek Exit #108 on same route for <u>Horse Creek Covered Bridge</u>. At the bottom of the hill in town, make a left turn where there is a small sign:

←COVERED BRIDGE
1 MILE

This is Riverside Street. Go about 1 mile to Neal Lane then turn right for about ½-a-mile down hill to the narrow, 1-lane, bridge.

Here is Oregon's only standing true Kingpost design covered bridge. As with several covered bridges, its construction date is disputed. It is on a narrow, picturesque county road that crosses Myrtle Creek a little southeast of the city. It is a favorite for bike riders. The bridge is posted at **5-TON** weight limit. Photos are best during afternoon□

Name: **North Fork Yachats River** Lincoln County
Structure No.: 12037 *World Guide* 37-10-07
Type/year: Queenpost 1938
Length: 42 feet
Spans: North Fork Yachats River
Owner: Lincoln County
Nearest town: Yachats
Nearest main highway: No: 101

STATUS	
OPEN TO:	
VEHICLES	☑
WALKERS	☑
BIKERS	☑
Status subject to change	

→From Highway No. 101, follow Yachats River Road to the concrete bridge then turn left for about 2 miles.

During summer months, when the foliage is in full green, this is probably one of the most picturesque covered bridges in Oregon. In winter, its appearance can be pretty stark.

Although only 7 miles from the Pacific Ocean, the community it serves is isolated and this bridge is the only access in or out. The weather phenomenon here is not unlike several other places near the ocean for the Coast Range Mountains protect these areas from the damp, "stinking fogge"*

After a heavy truck crashed through a wornout approach in 1987, the bridge received a general overhaul in 1989 – new trusses, roof, approaches and siding. The bridge engineer, finishing the job, proclaimed in 1989, this little 42-foot bridge should last 50 years. Here is another covered bridge with sloping sides to protect the but-tresses from the weather. □

---

* Sir Francis Drake describing the Oregon Coast on his viewing of it, from his ship, in 1572. He never did land. Refer to bibliography for *Oregon's Salty Coast*.

—John Snook photo

Name: **Office** Lane County
World Guide 37-10-39
Type/year: Howe 1944 (1993)
Length: 180 feet

Spans: North Fork of Middle Fork of the Willamette River
Owner: Lane County
Nearest town: Westfir
Nearest main highway: No: 58

→From freeway (I-5) south of Eugene, take Oakridge Exit to Highway No. 58. Turn on Westridge Avenue about Milepost 31 and go to Westfir on the county road another 2+ miles to the bridge. Office Covered Bridge is wheelchair accessible.

This is the most massive as well as the longest covered bridge in Oregon. It is also probably the tallest. It was the first to be lighted.

The Westfir Lumber Company built the bridge for access between its mill and its office and its company town, Westfir, across the river, hence the name.

Office Covered Bridge was planned for steel girder construction in the middle of World War II. Even though the production of lumber had a high priority, steel was even higher. The War Production Board refused to issue a Priority for steel. What to do? Would the WPB allow a Priority for the firm to use its own product for the bridge? Yes it would. To compensate for no steel, the engineers decided on triple timber beams, extra chords and extra steel tension rods.

Office Covered Bridge was unique-looking to the eye in the early

Greenway Park Commemorative Model Covered Bridge

→At Interstate-5, take Highway No. 58 to Lowell. (Owned by City of Lowell)

This little pedestrian bridge, also called Cannon Street Bridge, was constructed by Robert Everly and community volunteers in 1988 to recognize Lowell's historic association with covered bridges. These include Lowell, Unity, Pengra, Parvin covered bridges. This model is 14 feet long and 8 feet wide. It is 12 feet tall and is supported with 2 x 6-inch Howe trusses. This bridge, in Greenway Park, spans an old drainage area that has been filled to eliminate mosquitoes. □

days because it was painted green. Most covered bridges were white but a few were rusty-red.

Because the bridge was very long, and was transited by loaded log trucks many times a day, safety to pedestrians was a paramount issue. Accordingly, the design engineers built a separate walking bridge that was attached to an outside wall. Although the pedestrian bridge had four, wide, windows, so walkers might not feel too claustrophobic in the long tunnel, because war-work was day and night, electricians installed incandescent lights throughout its length.

Note, in the picture, the high cut to the portal thus allowing very high-loaded log trucks access without bashing in the bridge ends.

A devastating fire leveled the lumber mill in the 1980's. Barricades and locks then closed the bridge.

In late 1992, the bridge was transferred from private to Lane County ownership on a tax foreclosure case. In 1993, substantial rebuilding was done in order to provide long-term preservation. Again open to vehicles, Office Covered Bridge has a load limit of 20 tons. The walkway, alongside the covered bridge, has been made wheel chair accessible. ◇

Name: **Parvin** Lane County
Structure No.: 19-1W-21 *World Guide* 37-20-19
Type/year: Howe 1921 (1986)
Length: 75 feet
Spans: Lost Creek
Owner: Lane County
Nearest town: Dexter
Nearest main highway: No: 58

STATUS	
OPEN TO:	
VEHICLES	☑
WALKERS	☑
BIKERS	☑
Status subject to change	

→From Interstate-5, south of Eugene, proceed on Highway No. 58 about 11 miles then turn on Lost Creek Road. Proceed about 2 miles then turn right on Rattlesnake Road. Go about 1/2 mile then turn south on Lost Valley Lane then into Parvin Road.

Some earlier years ago there was a covered bridge here that had been set up in the late 1880's, but it was being eaten by big worms and had to be replaced. The present covered bridge was constructed in 1921. It was closed to vehicles in 1974 when the highway was realigned but the historic bridge was open for walkers and bikers.

Lane County, recognizing the importance of historic covered bridges, rebuilt Parvin Covered Bridge to handle general traffic – load limit 10 tons – in 1986. □

Name: **Pass Creek** Douglas County
World Guide 37-10-02
Type/year: Howe 1925 (moved, rebuilt 1986)
Length: 61 feet
Spans: Pass Creek
Owner: City of Drain
Nearest town: Within City of Drain
Nearest highway: Junction Highways Nos. 38 / 99

STATUS	
OPEN TO:	
WALKERS	☑
BIKERS	☑
Status subject to change	

→From southbound Interstate-5, take Exit #162 then proceed about 7 miles into Drain on First Street. Cross "B" Street then see Civic Center complex at 2nd and West "A" Streets. Drive to the rear of the parking lot for closest access to the bridge.

→From northbound Interstate-5, take Exit #150 then go about 9 miles to Drain. In town, turn right at "A" Street then see Civic Center complex at 2nd and West "A" Streets. Drive to the rear of the parking lot for closest access to the bridge.

This bridge has been known as "Pass Creek" Covered Bridge, with a history dating from 1870 when an earlier structure was on a stage route between the Willamette Valley and Jacksonville. The present bridge may have been built in 1906 then underwent massive rebuild in 1925. The bridge was bypassed by a concrete span in 1981, then the covered bridge was left to deteriorate.

The people of the town of Drain loved "their bridge" and wanted to preserve it. Accordingly, after all the chips fell into the right places, the bridge was dismantled, parts of it replaced with new members, then reinstalled in the Civic Center Campus with beautiful park surroundings. In summer, the rich and thick foliage, depending on sun angle, sometimes obscures parts of the bridge to the frustration of photographers. ☐

—John Snook photo

Name: **Pengra** Lane County

Structure No.: 18-1W-32 *World Guide* 37-20-15
Type/year: Howe   1938   (1993)
Length: 120 feet
Spans: Fall Creek
Owner: Lane County
Nearest town: Jasper
Nearest main highway: Highway No. 22

STATUS	
OPEN TO:	
VEHICLES	☑
WALKERS	☑
BIKERS	☑
Status subject to change	

→From Interstate-5, at Springfield, take the road to Jasper (north side of the McKenzie River – Highway No. 22) then on Pengra Road proceed 4 miles to Little Falls Creek Road make a turn to the east for about 1/4-mile to Place Road where the bridge is about 100 yards to the south.

→Or, from Interstate-5 south of Eugene, take Highway No. 58 about 5 miles to Parkway Road then proceed north 3 miles to Jasper. Turn southeast for 4 miles on Jasper-Lowell Road to Place Road.

Also known as Fall Creek Covered Bridge, the present structure replaced an earlier span that stood nearby dating back to 1904. The lower chords, 14 x 18 x 126 feet, are the largest single-piece timbers cut for a bridge in Oregon. The upper chords are 14 x 18 x 98 feet. The Pengra Covered Bridge was bypassed, due to general deterioration, in 1979.

Burrell Smith, a member of the Covered Bridge Society of Oregon, wrote in the Springfield *News* (Apr. 17, 1993):

Forlornly it sits in the shadows of the surrounding fir trees, its approaches crumbling into the rushing torrent of Fall Creek ... once a thing of beauty and utility ... now the powers that be wonder what to do with it.

Pengra Covered Bridge, restored in 1994, is re-opened to traffic. □

Name: **Porter–Limpy Creek** Josephine County
World Guide No. 37-17-A
Type/year: Log stringer 1980
Length: 36 feet
Spans: Limpy Creek
Owner: Private
Nearest town: Grants Pass
Nearest main highway: No. 199

STATUS
OPEN TO:
VEHICLES ☑
WALKERS ☑
BIKERS ☑
Status subject to change

→From Interstate-5, drive through Grants Pass on 6th Street. Cross the Rogue River then turn right (signal) to Highway No. 199. Proceed 6.9 miles, cross Applegate River then make sharp right turn into River Bank Road. Drive 4½ miles to Limpy Creek Road. Turn left (west), proceed 2 miles to 1800 Limpy Creek Road. Bridge is on the right, about 100 feet down steep lane. For vehicles larger than autos, but under 9 feet 6 inch vertical clearance, cross the bridge then proceed up narrow gravel driveway to **Y**. Bear left, take concrete bridge back to main road.

Porter-Limpy Creek Covered Bridge is in foliage that hides bridge from the sun and from most photographers. It exists because Don Porter had built a plank bridge then, as he had excess lumber, he covered it. The roof is hand-split cedar shakes. The bridge, rated at 10 ton capacity on two piers, has open sides affording exciting views of the rushing creek as it roars under the structure in early spring.

This bridge replaces a fir plank bridge Porter put there in 1968. It rotted. He built his new bridge in about 30 days in 1980. He hired a "1-man sawmill" to fell his own fir trees. These were sawn into 3 x 12 planks at the site. Four, 36-foot logs became stringers. The bridge is 12-feet wide with 12-inch running planks. The logs and boards are No. 1 quality and weatherized. He re-treats the bridge and fumigates every two years. The portals are salvaged siding from a house dating back to about 1900. ☐

Picnicking
in the
covered bridge.
Coos County
provided
the tables.

Photos by (top) Bert Webber (Lower) Orville Erdman

Pioneers named the village "Remote" because it was "remote" from everything. Being so "remote," the Post Office Department decided the village needed its own Post Office so it too was named "Remote." That was in 1887. Any way one looks at its location, even today, the village is still "remote."

Name: **Remote** Coos County
Structure No.: 4037 *World Guide* 37-06-09
Type/year: Howe   1921
Length: 65 feet
Spans: Sandy Creek
Owner: Coos County
Nearest town: Remote
Nearest main highway: No. 42

→From Interstate-5, take Highway No. 42 about 30 miles west of Roseburg to the village of Remote. The bridge is on the right within a few feet of the highway.

This is one of those several covered bridges that had more than one name. As the bridge straddles Sandy Creek, the bridge carried the creek's name.

The highway once passed through the bridge and in front of the village general store, but realignment of the highway in 1949, now separates the two.

This is considered a medium-length span, but because the covered bridge carried all the traffic between the coast and Roseburg, including heavily loaded logging trucks, the design engineers used crossed Howe trusses to provide added support. The bridge has wide and tall windows therefore visitors can easily see the unique construction.

The Remote Covered Bridge serves as a dedicated Coos County park and is open for picnics as well as walkers and bikers. On rainy days, it affords protection from rain during rest stops. □

East Creek private covered bridge in Tillamook County was dismantled some years ago. Its "garage doors" guaranteed the privacy of the owner..
—Author collection

Name: **Ritner Creek** Polk County

Structure No.: 1251 *World Guide* 37-27-01
Type/year: Howe 1927 (Moved and rebuilt 1976)
Length: 75 feet
Spans: Ritner Creek
Owner: Polk County
Nearest town: Pedee
Nearest main highway: No. 223

STATUS	
OPEN TO:	
VEHICLES	☑
WALKERS	☑
BIKERS	☑
Status subject to change	

→From Interstate-5, enter Salem and go through the city on Highway No. 22 to the Willamette River, and cross it following signs for Dallas – 17 miles. Then turn south on Highway No. 223 for another 12 miles passing through the village of Pedee (pron: PED-dee)* then go for another 3 miles to bridge.

Ritner Creek Covered Bridge was determined to be a hazard to users because it was too narrow, and traffic much too heavy, and faster than the 1927-era Model T Fords it was intended to carry, so it was ordered to be replaced in 1976. This was the last covered bridge to serve on a primary state highway. At one time, neighbors mounted their mail boxes in the bridge, but complaints and arguments between vehicles and pedestrians brought this practice to a stop.

The people voted a one-time tax to save the bridge and to provide a wayside park only 60 feet away. The little park, with its centerpiece, is one of the most photogenic covered bridge scenes in Oregon. □

---

* Refer to biblio for *Oregon Names How To Say Them and Where Are They Located?*

78

Name: **Roaring Camp** Douglas County
World Guide 37-10-11
Type/year: Howe 1929 (Re-built – steel 1995)
Length: 88 feet
Spans: Elk Creek
Owner: Private
Nearest town: Drain
Nearest main highway: Highway No. 38

STATUS	
OPEN TO:	
VEHICLES	☑
WALKERS	☑
BIKERS	☑
Status subject to change	

→From southbound Interstate-5, take Exit #162 then proceed about 7 miles into Drain. →From northbound Interstate-5, take Exit #150 then go about 9 miles to Drain. In Drain, visit pass Creek Covered bridge, which see in this book. To get to Roaring Camp Covered Bridge, take Highway No. 38 westward from Drain for 6.5 miles to an unmarked private road on the (south) left. See the bridge a few hundred feet down the road.

> **The bridge shown was replaced in 1995 with a steel span.**

Roaring Camp Covered Bridge benefits a few residents and the Kelly Green Nursery on a private road west of Drain. It got its unique name because nearby, in the early days, was the Roaring Camp Roadhouse. This old bridge has a couple of other names: Lancaster Bridge and Elk Creek Bridge. An official State

Report listed this covered bridge as "a working private bridge in sad shape...," but that was about 1990. In the next few years, the deadly disease of deterioration set in thus by December 1994, while some men were looking at the bridge's condition, one of them slipped and fell through a rotten 6-inch thick board.

The authors determined on the visit there on February 4th, 1995, that probably the worst section had been the wooden approach ramp on the highway end. This section was dismantled and replaced with a heavy, planked, walking lane but now the entire bridge has been replaced. The HISTORIC PLACE marker earlier installed at the highway, for public awareness, has been removed. (See the picture on page 10.)

A spokesman told the author that it would cost "about $450,000 to repair the bridge but only about $250,000 to put up a steel span." The steel work was completed in summer 1995. ◇

> While scurrying through the under-
> brush seeking good camera angles,
> be aware this is TICK country.

Temporary plank walkway at Roaring Camp Covered Bridge replaced original vehicle ramp. This ramp is now gone.
—Bert Webber photo

Name: **Rochester** Douglas County

Structure No. 1893 *World Guide* No. 37-10-04

Type/year: Howe 1933 (1969)

Length: 80 feet

Spans: Calapooya River

Owner: Douglas County

Nearest town: Sutherlin

Nearest main highway: No. 138

STATUS	
OPEN TO:	
VEHICLES	☑
WALKERS	☑
BIKERS	☑
Status subject to change	

→From Interstate-5, take Exit #138 at Sutherland and follow Highway No. 138 westerly for about 1½ miles then turn north on Stearns Road. Go about 1/2-mile to junction with Rochester Bridge Road. Turn left, see the bridge straight ahead, on a curve. Park well off this 2-lane roadway for safety.

One of the remarkable features of Rochester Covered Bridge is the cathedral tops to the windows. Another is that the bridge was at one time seemingly in great risk of being burned, by county road crews, to get rid of it. But local folks who loved their bridge, posted armed guards which convinced the county commissioners of their earnestness in keeping the bridge. Restored, the bridge takes local traffic but has a posted 5-ton load limit. □

Highway level

Very short very
steep approach ramp

Bridge deck level

Rock O' the Range
Covered Bridge
is north of Bend
on Highway No. 97

—Bert Webber photos

Name: **Rock O' The Range** Deschutes County
World Guide 37-09-X1
Type/year: Timber Deck Beam and Girder   1963
Length: 42 feet
Spans: Swalley Irrigation Canal
Owner: Private
Nearest town: Bend
Nearest main highway: No. 97

STATUS	
OPEN TO:	
VEHICLES	☑
WALKERS	☑
BIKERS	☑
Status subject to change	

→Rock O' The Range Covered Bridge in on Highway 97 just north of Mountain View Mall about 3 miles north of the city. As the bridge sits low, considering the elevation of the highway, watch closely for BOWERLY ROAD marker or drivers may miss the bridge.

This bridge was called the Bowerly Road Covered Bridge, or the Swalley Canal Covered Bridge by some who use it. It is the only covered bridge in Central or Eastern Oregon that is open both for vehicles and pedestrians. The only reason it's here is that a rancher, who was also a land developer, liked covered bridges and asked his contractor to build one.

Rock O' The Range Covered Bridge straddles the Deschutes Reclamation and Irrigation Canal, called the Swalley Canal, having been named for early settlers Ed and Elmira Swalley. They owned the water right in 1899 that allowed diversion of the Deschutes River into this ditch which runs intermittently in winter, and daily in summer's desert-like heat.

The bridge takes its design from a picture of a covered bridge on a calendar. Swalley Canal's covered bridge is a favorite of tourists. Interviews reveal this is because it is one-of-a-kind and the only one for over 100 miles in any direction the locals can show to visitors.

Douglas Fir was used for studs and 6-inch wide tongue-and-groove siding. The bridge has hand-split cedar shake roof. At a glance, the construction might lead some to think it is a Kingpost truss. But this bridge has only angled braces between the studs. With no trusses, it frequently gets only a scant smile from covered bridge purists.

There is no other bridge like this in Oregon

Rock O' The Range Covered Bridge is a one-lane bridge with wide plank runners for vehicles centered in its 14-feet width. The bridge rests on concrete piers and boasts a 25-ton limit. The cover on the bridge is supported by rafters. There are large rectangular "ribbon" windows running nearly the length of the bridge to provide illumination and an escape for lots of summer heat. There are deck-level windows that admit fresh cool air from the water below affording a natural convection cooling for the interior of the bridge.

Bowerly Road is a public road serving the population living on it. Deschutes County has declined to maintain the bridge declaring it is too small and a liability. Part of the challenge is believed to be that the bridge's deck is well below the grade of Highway No. 97, a mere few feet away from it. In driving over the edge of the highway onto the short graveled access to the bridge, vehicles can negotiate the dip (see sketch) at only about 5 miles per hour.

Although built with a 12-foot clearance, the ever increasing elevation of the highway with new pavement over new pavement through the years, has caused a severe dip for vehicles trying to get on the east end of the bridge. Trucks now must be limited to 9-feet, 1-inch clearance. Some unobservant truckers have crashed the east portal, which causes residents no end of frustration as they have to bear the costs of repairs which must be made by them. Just about everyone has taken a turn. (Fire Trucks, RV's and other large vehicles must enter the property in a round-about manner by another route.) □

Original Antelope Covered bridge, built in 1922. It spanned Antelope Creek east of Eagle Pont. The bridge was dismanatled and moved into town. See Eagle Point
—Jackson County Public Works

Name: Shimanek Linn County
Structure No,: 12965 *World Guide* 37-22-03
Type/year: Howe 1966
Length: 130 feet
Spans: Thomas Creek
Owner: Linn County
Nearest town: Scio
Nearest main highway: No. 226

STATUS	
OPEN TO:	
VEHICLES	☑
WALKERS	☑
BIKERS	☑
Status subject to change	

—Bert Webber photo

→From Scio, go east 2 miles on Highway No. 226 to Richardson Gap Road. Make a left turn and proceed 1 mile to the bridge.

The present bridge at this site is one of the youngest in Oregon but is the fifth span at this place on Richardson Gap County Road. Back in 1861, the first bridge here did not have a cover. Starting in 1904, and succeeding bridges, all had lids. These came along in 1924 and 1927. The 1921 bridge was built because the earlier one washed away in a flood. Again in 1927, a flood caused severe trauma to the bridge and it was declared unsafe. The new bridge was very badly damaged in the famous Columbus Day Storm of 1962 to where traffic was limited to a single lane and loads were reduced to a mere 2 tons. But the damage had been severe and the bridge was wrecked.

The present Shimanek (pron: shim-AWN-ik*) Covered Bridge has withstood the rains and floods but has met with a more modern type of distress. Some high school fellows, with their hot-rod cars, loved to race down the hill, hit the short, high-angled bridge approach at high speed. A car would become airborne – the object being to see how far it would "fly" before thudding to the deck. There were a number of wrecks then finally a fatal smash.

In 1990, the county built a new approach. The old one had never been any peril to drivers who observed the speed limit. Our camera was at the bridge during the final grading that eliminated the high-angle risk for those who might want to try it just one more time. The bridge was damaged in the 1996 flood but repairs were completed in 1997. ◇

* Refer to biblio for *Oregon Names, How To Say Them and Where Are They Located?*

Name: **Short** Linn County
ODOT No,: 14025 *World Guide* 37-22-09
Type/year: Howe 1945
Length: 105 feet
Spans: South Fork Santiam River
Owner: Linn County
Nearest town: Cascadia
Nearest main highway: No. 20

STATUS	
OPEN TO:	
VEHICLES	☑
WALKERS	☑
BIKERS	☑
Status subject to change	

→ From Interstate-5, Albany Exit, about 37 miles on Highway No. 20 to Cascadia. Turn on to High Deck Road. Find the bridge just a stone's throw distance.

For years this was known as Whisky Butte Covered Bridge for a prominent bump on the earth nearby. (*See* GREEN PETER TOPOGRAPH-IC MAP) Now named Short Covered Bridge, it handles regular traffic and is in good shape because of continuing servicing. In 1988, it had a major re-do of its beams, deck, roof, railings as well as new paint. There is some swimming here in the summer months but the water is claimed to be quite cool, which fishermen also enjoy. ☐

Name: **Stewart** Lane County
ODOT No,: 39C243   *World Guide* 37-20-28
Type/year: Howe   1930
Length: 60 feet

STATUS
OPEN TO:
  WALKERS ☑
  BIKERS   ☑
Status subject to change

Spans: Mosby Creek
Owner: Lane County
Nearest town: Cottage Grove
Nearest main highway: Interstate-5

→From Cottage Grove, drive about 3 miles by way of Mosby Creek Road, cross the railroad, then make a left turn. The bridge is where Mosby Creek Road and Garoutte Road cross.

This bridge was once known as Mosby Creek Covered Bridge – is 60-feet long built in 1930 – and should not be confused with "Mosby" Creek Covered Bridge - 90-feet long built in 1920 - both in Lane County (which see). The Christmas Flood of 1964 did severe damage then the roof collapsed under heavy snow in 1968. After decades of damaging incidents, severe weather included, Stewart Covered Bridge was bypassed with a concrete span just a few yards away in the 1980's. The bridge was repainted as part of Lane County's preservation policy in 1987 then it was maintained just for bikers and walkers. High water during the December 1996 flood piled logs and whole trees against the bridge. In addition, the high water broke off new boards from the sides that had been replaced only one year earlier. The bridge was again repaired in 1997 ◇

—Bert Webber photo

Name: **Tissot Memorial**   Josephine County
World Guide No. 37-17-B
Type/Year: Timber deck girder   1990
Length: 22 feet 3 inches
Spans: Wolf Creek
Owner: Private
Nearest town: Within village of Wolf Creek
Nearest main highway: No. 99

STATUS	
OPEN TO:	
VEHICLES	☑
WALKERS	☑
BIKERS	☑
Status subject to change	

→From Interstate-5 take Wolf Creek Exit. In the village, look for large Texaco station. The bridge is immediately north of the station on east side of highway – faces highway – has street number 441 centered over portal. In summer, most of bridge is hidden in foliage. Wheel-chair accessible.

This unique privately built and owned covered bridge serves the residence of Merle and Susan Converse whose home is the two-story house behind. The house was built between 1870-76. The property has been in the family since 1927 and this couple, with their family, has lived in this modernized century old structure since 1977.

There has always been a bridge of some kind here. In the 1950's, there was a "floating bridge" built of planks on logs with guy wires tied to stout trees upstream. When the creek rose in high water, the bridge rose with it. This survived the 1955 flood but the famous 1964 flood washed it out. When Merle Converse arrived, there was a log bridge over the creek that had apparently been put there by a clan of

—Bert Webber photo
Tissot Memorial Covered bridge appears undressed
in winter when the leaves are gone from the trees,

counter-culturists. They had squatted in the house for several years. It was about 1984 when a heavy propane truck, that had crossed the bridge many times, finally crashed through and landed in Wolf Creek. Following that incident, Converse built a bridge of 8 x 8-inch untreated mill logs covered with 2 x 6-inch planks mounted on edge with spacers to let rain drain into the creek. In spite of these measures, that bridge rotted.

> Here is a recent covered bridge that has been con-
> structed completely of recycled materials. The stringers
> are weatherized 7 x 26 inch x 24-feet long fir. They came
> from an old mill. Some of the siding came from a donkey
> engine shed that was dismantled at a mill near Glendale.
> Other siding is from an 1870 barn. The bridge's roof is
> second-hand corrugated sheet iron from a saw mill.

He decided if he wanted to keep the rain off his bridge, the only answer was a covered bridge. Accordingly, he built the Tissot Memorial Covered Bridge. This remembers his late grandfather, Clarence Louis Tissot.

There is about 7-feet between the bottom of the bridge and the creek in summer and "considerably less clearance" during winter storms. The creek boasts trout and, although not classed as an "official" breeding place for salmon, wayward salmon have been seen there.

Visitors should park on the highway side of the bridge as there is only the narrow private driveway beyond. Best camera time is mid-afternoon in summer. □

Name: **Unity** Lane County
Structure No,: 14721 *World Guide* 37-20-17
Type/year: Howe 1936
Length: 90 feet
Spans: Fall Creek
Owner: Lane County
Nearest town: Lowell
Nearest main highway: No. 58

STATUS	
OPEN TO:	
VEHICLES	☑
WALKERS	☑
BIKERS	☑
Status subject to change	

→From Interstate-5 south of Eugene, take Highway No. 58 to Lowell then the Lowell-Unity county road about 2 miles to the bridge.

Unity Covered Bridge was also known as Fall Creek Covered Bridge. The "Unity" community here, should not be confused with the town of Unity in Baker County which has no covered bridge.

Two covered bridges served here for many years. The original, 129-feet long (Howe) was finally limited to bikes and walkers in 1935 due to deterioration. But further decay stopped even foot traffic in 1953. In the meantime, the present covered bridge was installed about three quarters of a mile upstream and opened in 1936.

The uniqueness of Unity Covered Bridge is the long window along the bridge's east side so drivers can see on-coming vehicles. The window has its own "roof" in an effort to shield motorist's eyes from the sun and to try to keep some of the rain out. ◇

Name: **Warner Canyon** Lake County —John Snook photo
World Guide 37-19-X-1
Type/year: Railroad flatcar 1985
Length: 50 feet
Spans: dry gulch

Owner: Private
Nearest town: Lakeview
Nearest main highway: No. 140

→From Lakeview, go north on Highway 395 to the junction with Highway No. 140. Turn right into No. 140 and drive about 1½ miles. The Warner Canyon Covered bridge can be seen on the left from the highway. Drivers should continue past the bridge looking for a suitable place to park as there are no turnouts close by.

This covered span is presently Lake county's sole claim to having a covered bridge. Bob Pepperling owned the land and wanted to subdivide and sell a parcel on the other side of a dry gulch. He built the bridge as an access to that parcel.

For $2,500, he bought a flat car from Southern Pacific Company in Klamath Falls, then he paid another $1,000 to have it delivered to his site. The bridge is 9-feet wide and has an overhead clearance of 10-feet. He finished the deck with 4 x 12-inch boards and used 3 x 12-inch stringers. The roof is covered with hand-split shakes. For the sides of his covered bridge, he used rough sawn cedar boards and batten into which he cut two windows on each side for light. The approaches to the bridge were never finished.

At last report, Pepperling had taken up cattle ranching in Canada and his property, with the bridge, is for sale. □

Name: **Wayne A. Perry**   Josephine County
World Guide No. 37-17-C
Type/Year: Modified Kingpost   1991
Length: 57 feet
Spans: West Fork Williams Creek
Owner: Private
Nearest Town: Williams
Nearest main highway: No. 238

STATUS	
OPEN TO:	
VEHICLES	☑
WALKERS	☑
BIKERS	☑
Status subject to change	

→Depending on route through Medford, trip is about 33 miles to the bridge.
From Interstate-5, North Medford Exit, turn right taking the main wide street
into town to McAndrews Road (Signal). Turn right, pass over the viaduct and
go to North Ross Lane (Arterial Stop). Turn left, proceed to West Main Street
- Highway No. 238 (Signal). Turn right, drive to and through Jacksonville. (At
Ruch (pron *Roosch*) one can turn left onto Applegate Road to reach McKee
Covered Bridge.) Otherwise continue on Highway No. 238 to Provolt. Turn
left at store, now going south to Williams. Pass through Williams to Cedar
Flat Road then look for Street No. 2475. Enter narrow unpaved lane and
proceed 1/4-mile to Wayne A. Perry Covered Bridge.

The Wayne A. Perry Covered Bridge was completed on
Valentines Day 1991. It was a gift to the builder's wife, Jean.
Perry also calls the structure the "Bridge To The Heart."

Jean Perry had always wanted a covered bridge so her husband, Wayne, a building contractor, decided to build one for her.

Finding an appropriate site was not difficult, as they lived just a few yards from the creek and the land on which the bridge has been built is their own.

The trusses are modified 2-panel Kingposts of Perry's own design to support the roof and the housing. He used 12/12 pitch rafters then covered the bridge with a sheet metal roof. The supports are exposed buttresses, 3 on each side. There are 4 roofed windows with elliptical heads.The bridge is rated at 15 tons limit.

There is restricted turn-around space at the bridge but large RV's and trailers are not encouraged.

The Wayne A. Perry Covered Bridge was featured in Vol. 13, No. 2, Summer 1992 edition of *The Bridge Tender*. Perry framed a copy of the article and it is mounted inside the west portal for visitors to read. The best picture-making time is early afternoon in summer. □

No longer standing Wagon Covered Bridge over Santiam River at Lebanon was three bridges hooked together – the center span and two short approach spans.
—Author collection

Name: **Weddle** Linn County
Structure No.: 12935   *World Guide* 37-22-05
Type/year: Howe   1937   (Moved and rebuilt 1990)
Length: 120 feet
Spans: Ames Creek
Owner: City of Sweet Home
Nearest town: Within City of Sweet Home
Nearest main highway: No. 20

STATUS
OPEN TO:
WALKERS ☑
BIKERS ☑
Status subject to change

→From Interstate-5, take Highway No. 20 to Sweet Home then make a right turn into 12th Street, at the signal, and drive 2 blocks then go in front of the City Hall to Kalmia Street. Drive 2 more blocks and note a curve in the street but keep going to Sankey Park and see the bridge – the larger of two covered bridges in the park.

Although this span had traditionally been called the Devaney Covered Bridge, the county commissioners changed the name. It was bypassed in favor of a concrete bridge in 1980 but the old covered bridge, then 43 years sold, was kept for bikers and walkers. Finally, in 1987, the bridge was ordered down. Workers took the order literally and with wrecking-ball efficiency, the covered bridge, except for the stout trusses, was reduced to rubble then burned.

A number of interested groups, including the Covered Bridge Society of Oregon, wanted to rebuild it. The Cascade Forest Resource Center was organized for the task and received vital assistance from the Jordan Bridge Company, the committee from Stayton that had re-built the Jordan Covered Bridge there.

Substantial physical labor on the reconstruction was done by the Building Trades Class from Sweet Home High School, supervised by the teacher, Ben Dahlenburg. Some money from the Oregon State Lottery (Economic Development) was contributed. The work was completed in 1989. Enjoy! □

Name: **Wendling** Lane County   —John Snook photo

Structure No.: 39C174 *World Guide* 37-20-36

Type/year: Howe   1938

Length: 60 feet

Spans: Mill Creek

Owner: Lane County

Nearest town: Marcola

Nearest main highway: No. 20

STATUS	
OPEN TO:	
VEHICLES	☑
WALKERS	☑
BIKERS	☑
Status subject to change	

➔From Interstate-5 take the Springfield exit and go through town on 14th Street (Marcola Road). In Marcola, make right turn into Wendling Road to the bridge.

In 1938, when Lane County went on a binge for building covered bridges, this was one of four constructed. The others were Goodpasture, Pengra and Earnest. The basic plans are the same, but each bridge has uniquenesses that become apparent when studying side-by-side photographs.

This is a covered bridge that in a summer, with full foliage surrounding it, is a typical, picturesque, Oregon setting. A feature of Wendling Covered Bridge, as well as Earnest and Pengra, is the ribbon windows (vents) running the length of the bridge near the top. Summers can get quite hot in the Willamette Valley and many think this feature is to let the heat and moisture out. This is true. ☐

Widing Covered Bridge

↑ Frame construction
→ **1990 view**
—Bert Webber photos
← **1970 view**
—Author collection

The bridge, and all the greenery, has been demolished by developers

Name: **Widing** Multnomah County

World Guide 37-26-X1
Type/year: Frame stringer 1965
Length: 38 feet, 10 inches   1 span
Spans: East end Columbia Lake
Owner: Private
Nearest town: Within City of Portland
Nearest main highway: Marine Drive

> STATUS:
> REMOVED

→The area can be viewed from the eastbound lane just east of the 121st St. N.E. marker, but any glance is hazardous due to usual heavy traffic on this 2-lane "speedway" road.

There are two approaches from Interstate-5. The northerly is to take the Marine Drive Exit near the Interstate Bridge and stay on that Drive to the 121st St. N.E. marker. The other is to leave I-5 at Banfield Freeway (I-84) and go east to 122nd Street N.E. Exit. Take 122nd Street north to Marine Drive then turn (west) left and watch, carefully, for the 121st St. N.E. marker. If one drives past that marker, he has gone too far !

> **Widing Covered Bridge was sometimes referred to as Oregon's Lost Covered Bridge because most folks, including nearby residents, didn't know it was there.**

The late Glenn Aren Widing liked covered bridges so he decided to build one that he could see from his mansion. The bridge, on the former driveway to his estate, crossed the east end of Columbia Lake. That swampy area has now been reclaimed by developers.

The bridge frame and sides were in deplorable condition when the authors were there. The deck of 2 x 10-inch crossplanks, on which were running strips of 6 x 8 x 38 feet long, were apparently in good shape due to limited usage. Access is now thwarted as the developers tore down the bridge.

The land, which includes the location of the bridge, has now been developed. There is no trace of the former covered bridge. ◇

—John Snook photo

Name: **Wildcat Creek** Lane County

Structure No.: 39C446 *World Guide* 37-26-X1

Type/year: Howe 1925   (1990)

Length: 75 feet

Spans: Wildcat Creek

Owner: Lane County

Nearest town: Walton

Nearest main highway: No. 126

STATUS	
OPEN TO:	
VEHICLES	☑
WALKERS	☑
BIKERS	☑
Status subject to change	

> The name of this bridge is expressed in either of two ways: <u>Wildcat</u>, and <u>Wild</u> <u>Cat</u>. The *Geographic Names Information System – Oregon* lists it as one word.

→Follow Highway No. 126 west from Eugene for about 24 miles to Siuslaw Road then, taking it only about 200 feet to Austa Road. Go under the highway and railroad overpass to the bridge, about 3/4-mile.

Also called the Austa Covered Bridge, this picturesque Wildcat Covered Bridge has seen a lot of traffic in its time and for years was restricted to autos with a 2-ton limit. However the bridge was fixed in 1990 and now handles 20 tons. The bridge is at a curve in the narrow road and has been provided with a low-level "window" on the east wall. This way, drivers on the bridge can see any approaching traffic.

The bridge is near the confluence with the Siuslaw River and provides access to a public boat ramp highly favored by fishermen. □

—John Snook photo

Name: **Wimer** Jackson County

Structure No. 29C211 *World Guide* 37-156-05

Type/year: Queenpost 1927 (1962)

Length: 85 feet

Spans: Evans Creek

Owner: Jackson County

Nearest town: Wimer

Nearest main highway: Interstate-5

STATUS	
OPEN TO:	
VEHICLES	☑
WALKERS	☑
BIKERS	☑
Status subject to change	

→Leave the freeway (I-5) at Rogue River Exit and drive north, through the town, for 7 miles on East Evans Creek Road. After driving through the covered bridge, you emerge in the center of the village.

Wimer Covered bridge is another with confused dates as to its origin with some records showing a bridge was installed here as early as 1892, then replaced in 1927 with the present span. In the early 1960's, the bridge was so shaky, it was declared "endangered" but the local people, who loved their bridge, were able, in 1962, to have it fixed.

A decade later, Wimer Covered Bridge was again in trouble so it was closed until general restoration could happen. The bridge, which is right in the center of the village, was reopened, with great enthusiasm, for the centennial of the town in 1986. The unique WIMER name signs posted on the bridges portals – white letters on maroon – are said to have been salvaged from an old gas station. These are the only signs of the type to be found on any of the covered bridges in Oregon.

Wimer Covered Bridge is the only covered bridge in Jackson County open to motor vehicles. ☐

Covered Bridges Listed By County

Benton: Harris Hayden Irish Bend

Coos: Remote

Deschutes: Rock O' The Range

Douglas: Cavitt Dave Birtch Horse Cr Milo Mott Memorial Neal Cr Pass Cr Roaring Camp Rochester

Gilliam: China Ditch

Jackson: Eagle Point Lost Cr McKee Wimer

Josephine: Grave Cr Porter–Limpy Cr Tissot Memorial Wayne A. Perry

Lake: Warner Canyon

Lane: Belknap Centennial Chambers Coyote Currin Deadwood Dorena Earnest Goodpasture Lake Cr Lowell Mosby Office Parvin Pengra Stewart Unity Wendling Wildcat

Lincoln: Chitwood Drift Cr Fisher N.Fork Yachats

Linn: Bohemian Hall Cascadia Crawfordsville Dahlenburg Gilkey Hannah Hoffman Joel Whittemore Larwood Shimanek Short Weddle

Marion: Gallon House Jordan

Multnomah: Cedar Crossing Widing

Polk: Fourtner Ritner Cr

Some Covered Bridges Of The Past....

—Fred Kildow collection

—Fred Kildow collection

Schooner Creek covered bridge on highway
101 at Taft (top) was replaced by concrete
bridge when this main highway was widened
after World War II. (Lower) Carver bridge over
Clackamas River.

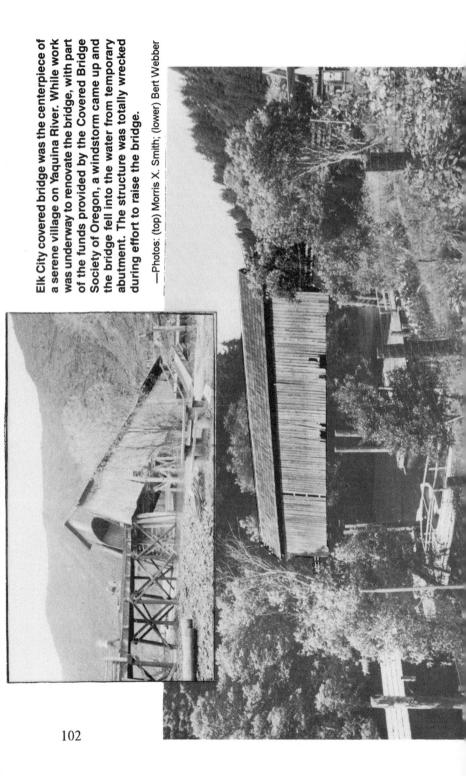

Elk City covered bridge was the centerpiece of a serene village on Yaquina River. While work was underway to renovate the bridge, with part of the funds provided by the Covered Bridge Society of Oregon, a windstorm came up and the bridge fell into the water from temporary abutment. The structure was totally wrecked during effort to raise the bridge.

—Photos: (top) Morris X. Smith; (lower) Bert Webber

The card reads:
Roseburg Feb. 14, '09
In the spring of 1906, I kicked the middle plank off this bridge so people could see down the river. Yesterday when I bought some cards, I told the clerk and he said a man told the same story a few days ago. Who lied? This is near Prospect.

—Bert Webber photos

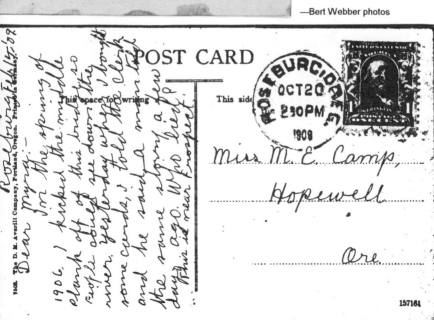

103

—Fred Kildow collection

—Bert Webber photo

Old covered bridge on Tillamook-McMinnville Stage Road shows four spans, one covered. (Right) Mapleton bridges, new and old. The concrete span was not yet open when the authors visited there in 1974.

Which Bridge is Which?
The *World Guide* Number System

Because bridge types, names of streams bridges cross, local names given to bridges, and other identifying factors are often the same, it became necessary for a scheme of identification to be established where each bridge would be clearly different from any other. Accordingly, the *World Guide Covered Bridge Numbering System* was developed. Credit for this international identification system is given to Philip and Betsy Clough. This system was adopted by the National Society for the Preservation of Covered Bridges.

For use in the United States, three elements are used. These are 00 00 00. The first two digits identify the states in alphabetical order with 01 assigned to Alabama; 05 is assigned to California; 37 is Oregon.

The second block is for county identification. In Oregon, Baker County is 01. As there are no known covered bridges in that county, "01" is not found in this book. Benton County is 02. There are several covered bridges in Benton County thus 02 is found here.

The third set of double-digits identifies a specific bridge within a county. It is considered that some bridges may be dismantled and moved; others may be lost in floods or by fire. If a bridge is destroyed, the number stays with the bridge. A number once assigned, is never reassigned if its bridge is lost.

A test of the system will happen in Oregon shortly. In December 1994, the Jordan Covered Bridge burned. After the fire was out, the the Stayton Fire Department bulldozed the remains into a heap and reburned the debris into ashes. By this action was the bridge *lost* ? Did the bridge's number also go down in the flames ?

The 90-feet long stringers that supported the bridge, were reportedly undamaged by the fire. If the restoration committee rebuilds on existing stringers, then, apparently, the *World Guide* number was not lost. Will rebuilding on original stringers keep the original number?

There are several bridges with numbers that do not have official *World Guide* recognition (remember – 00-00-00) because these are not considered "true truss supported." A local private covered bridge might have a number as 37-09-X1 (Rock O' The Range) or 37-19-X1 (Warner Canyon). Then there is Porter–Limpy Creek with 37-17-A, Tissot Memorial 37-17-B and so on.

While the numbering system is essential for positively identifying every bridge as different from any other covered bridge, the friendly folks who just enjoy driving around looking at the nostalgic wonder of covered bridges, don't seem to let themselves get bogged down in technical nomenclature. □

Glossary

Abutment   An abutment supports the end of a single or multi-span structure and, in general, supports the approach embankment. Usually of rock, concrete or timber, *see also:* Piling.

Approach   The passageway from the roadbed onto the bridge. Often of wood in older bridges, now concrete or asphalt.

Bridge   A structure that allows continuous passage over water, road or valley. Generally carries a path, road or railroad, but may also carry power lines or pipe lines. An observer quipped that since highways are not pretty to look at and bridges are, the only reason for highways is to connect the bridges.

Buttress   An abutting pier that braces a wall.

Ca.   *Circa,* an estimated date.

Chord   A main horizontal member of a truss. Traditional covered bridges often have upper and lower chords.

Covered bridge   A structure (*see:* Bridge), usually timber but recently a few are being built on bases of salvaged railroad flat cars, with a roof and usually siding as protection from weather.

Daylighting   Provision in design of covered bridges for allowing light to enter the closed bridge by various designs or sizes of windows.

Dead load   Weight of a bridge — gross weight.

Deck   The roadway surface of a bridge.

Diagonal   The timber affixed on an angle that connects upper and lower chords.

End post   A diagonal installed at either end of a truss.

Flying buttress   *(Arc-boutant)* A prop that arises from a support and ends against another part of a structure to provide added strength to the structure. In slang, sometimes called "out-riggers."

Foundation   The abutment that supports ends of a bridge. *See also:* Abutment.

Hewn timber   Finished surface of log shaped by hand tools applied here primarily in shaping a log into a truss.

Lower chord   The lower truss, also called stringer or girder in covered bridges.

National Register   The *National Register of Historic Places* is a list (in book form) maintained by the National Park Service of the nation's cultural resources deemed worthy of preservation. The list includes districts, archeological and historical sites, buildings, structures (including covered bridges) and selected objects of national, state and local worthiness.

ODOT	Oregon Department of Transportation.
Pier	A structure intended to support the ends of the spans of a multi-span superstructure at an intermediate location between abutments. *See also:* Abutment.
Piling	Logs (poles) driven into the ground on which a bridge or approach is mounted.
Pony truss	A low through truss that has no overhead or enclosing truss work. The word "pony" means something smaller than standard.
Portal	Entrance to a bridge, especially a through truss or arch.
Portal message	A plaque mounted above the entrance portal of a bridge on which indicia about the bridge, possibly the name of the bridge, has been affixed.
Portal weatherboard	Wood cover affixed inside a portal intended to shield lower truss and its joints from water splattered on wet days by vehicles.
Rafter	Any of the parallel beams that support a roof. In covered bridges, rafters form the peak in center of roof, the opposite ends resting on the top truss.
Span	Distance between abutments; the deck, if the deck is separate from approaches.
Spandrel	The area between the exterior curves of an arch and the roadway.
Stringer	Supporting timber under bridge deck.
Sway brace	*See:* Flying buttress.
Tie rod	Metal tension rods used in vertical position holding upper and lower chords in correct positions. These rods are threaded and can be adjusted if need be. Queenpost and Howe trusses use tension (tie) rods.
Through	Form of bridge in which traffic moves through the framework of a bridge.
Truss	A bridge with a framework of members, forming a triangle or system of triangles to support the weight of the bridge as well as passing loads.
Tuning tie rods	Periodic adjustment of tie rods (tension rods) to maintain specified tension between upper and lower trusses.
Upper chord	The upper truss, also called stringer or girder in covered bridges.

Master List of Inventoried Bridges in Oregon For Those Counties With Covered Bridges A Covered Bridge as defined for use in this book is any bridge over which there is a roof except on golf courses		
County	No. of Bridges†	No. of Covered Bridges
Benton	14	3
Coos	10	1
Deschutes	4	1
Douglas	35	9
Gilliam	1	1
Jackson	24	4
Josephine	16	4
Lake	5	1
Lane	62	19
Lincoln	14	4
Linn	27	12
Marion	31	2
Multnomah	74	2
Polk	12	2
		65

† Extracted from *Historic Highway Bridges of Oregon*. The inventory was published in 1986. The number of covered bridges (column 3) is corrected to February 1995 however, the existence and locations of some privately owned covered bridges are difficult to determine and some may have been inadvertently omitted. If readers know of covered bridges, other than on golf courses, in Oregon not found in this book, a letter to the publisher (address on page *iv*) will be appreciated. –Editor

Bibliography

Adams, Kramer A. *Covered Bridges of the West.* Howell-North. 1963.

Black, John and Marguerite. *Ruch and the Upper Applegate Valley (An Oregon Documentary).* Webb Research Group. 1989.

Cockrell, Bill and Nick Cockrell. *Roofs Over Rivers.* Touchstone. 1978.

_____. *Roofs Over Rivers. The New Guide to Oregon's Covered Bridges.* Oregon Sentinel. 1989.

Covered Bridges of Douglas County. Roseburg Visitors & Convention Bureau. 1993.

Ellsworth, Christine. "1990 Oregon Safari" in *Covered Bridge Topics.* Vol. XLVIII. No. 4. The National Society for the Preservation of Covered Bridges. Fall, 1990.

Geographic Names System (Oregon). Branch of Geographic Names, U. S. Geological Survey [unfinished] Dec. 1992.

A Guide to Covered Bridges in Lane County, Oregon. Lane County Public Works. 1995.

Helbock, Richard W. *Oregon Post Offices 1847 - 1982.* LaPosta. 1982.

Helsel, Bill. *World Guide to Covered Bridges.* The National Society for the Preservation of Covered Bridges. 1989.

Lane, Oscar P. *World Guide to Covered Bridges.* The National Society for the Preservation of Covered Bridges. 1972.

McCoy, Imogene W. "Charming Americana Covered Bridge Spans Canal Over Original Water Right in Central Oregon," in *Covered Bridge Topics.* Apr. 8, 1968.

Merriam, Lawrence C. Jr. *Oregon's Highway Park System 1921-1989...Including Historical Overview and Park Directory.* Oregon State Parks. Salem. 1992.

Nelson, Lee H. *A Century of Oregon Covered Bridges 1851-1952.* Oregon Historical Society. 1976.

"Over Johnson Creek - County to Construct Covered Bridge," in *Oregonian.* Sep. 30, 1981. p. B1.

"Peedee Kids Save Historic Polk Covered Bridge," in *Oregon Journal.* May 20, 1976. p.17.

Ricketts, E. G. *Covered Bridges in Oregon.* Office of the Bridge Testing Engineer, Oregon State Highway Dept. 1938 [updated with footnotes to Aug. 7, 1969].

Smith, Dwight A., James B. Norman and Pieter T. Dykman. *Historic Highway Bridges of Oregon.* Oregon Dept. of Transportation 1986.

Webber, Bert. "Covered Bridge Loss Draws Blast By State Historians," in *Oregon Journal.* Apr. 6, 1974.

Webber, Bert. *Oregon Names How To Say Them and Where Are They Located ?* Webb Research Group. 1995.

Webber, Bert and Margie. *Oregon Covered Bridges; An Oregon Documentary in Pictures.* Webb Research Group. 1991.

About the Authors

Bert Webber's first encounter with an Oregon covered bridge was while he was riding a Greyhound bus on a winter day in 1941 when he was on a trip from San Francisco to Camp Clatsop on the Oregon Coast. That bridge crossed Grave Creek in Josephine County.

In the following decades he has photographed many dozens of covered bridges. Some of the pictures are included here.

Margie and Bert Webber with their "Field Research Unit"

Bert is a research-photojournalist, has authored or contributed to around eighty books most about some aspect of the Oregon Country. He holds a Bachelor's Degree in Journalism from Whitworth College. He also earned the Master of Library Science Degree from study at Portland State University and the University of Portland. He was a school librarian for a number of years as well as owner of retail and wholesale businesses. He has always done some writing but turned to full-time writing when he left librarianship in 1970.

His aim is to write in language easily understood but with authority so his books can be useful to Reference Librarians.

Bert Webber is a member of the Covered Bridge Society of Oregon. He is cited in *Who's Who in the West, Who's Who in America, Who's Who in the World* and in *Contemporary Authors.* He was awarded the *Decree of Merit* in *Men of Achievement* at the International Biographical Centre, Cambridge, England.

One of Webber's fun-time hobbies is playing the Euphonium in the Southern Oregon Concert Band where he also serves as Vice President for Administrative Affairs on the Board of Control.

Margie Webber is a retired Registered Nurse who earned her baccalaureate degree in Nursing at the University of Washington. After a variety of positions in Washington and Oregon in her professional field, she retired to become a co-author, with her husband, on many books about Oregon. For the present book, she served as Senior Editor. She often makes pictures which appear in the various books.

The Webber's make their home in Oregon's Rogue River Valley where there are half-a-dozen covered bridges within a few minutes drive. They have four children and eight grand children.